THREE STUDIES IN SHELLEY

THREE STUDIES IN SHELLEY

AND

AN ESSAY ON NATURE IN

WORDSWORTH AND MEREDITH

BY

ARCHIBALD T. STRONG

ARCHON BOOKS
1968

FIRST PUBLISHED 1921
OXFORD UNIVERSITY PRESS
REPRINTED 1968 WITH PERMISSION
IN AN UNALTERED AND UNABRIDGED EDITION

210795

SBN: 208 00665 6
LIBRARY OF CONGRESS CATALOG CARD NUMBER: 68-26936
PRINTED IN THE UNITED STATES OF AMERICA

TO

W. R. AND L. J. BOYCE GIBSON

PREFATORY NOTE

THE following studies of Shelley's poetry deal rather with its thought and symbolism than with its formal characteristics. Intrinsically, these characteristics are of the first importance: but they are less important for the purpose of the present inquiry, which chiefly aims at penetrating by different approaches as far as may be into Shelley's heart and mind. In this adventure, a certain unity of aim and method has been observed, or at least attempted. In one essay, it has been deemed necessary to discuss certain aspects of Shelley's character as displayed in certain episodes of his life. This has been done, not in order to furnish fresh 'chatter about Harriet'—or Elizabeth or Emilia—but solely for the light which Shelley's psychology sheds upon his poetry. In the last essay, an attempt has been made to compare the thought and outlook of the two who of all modern English poets have seen most deeply into the heart of Nature.

A. T. S.

June 20, 1920.

CONTENTS

THE FAITH OF SHELLEY

THE main tendencies of Shelley's social and religious belief are generally considered fairly obvious, and this in spite of the fact that his support and authority are claimed by thinkers of diametrically opposite tendencies. The rationalists hail him as an atheist or an Aufklärer, the transcendentalists as a Platonic idealist, the socialists as a practical reformer, and the mystics as the greatest of modern symbolists. Even his attitude toward Christianity, which is the least ambiguous article of his faith, has been oppositely interpreted. 'Had Shelley lived,' says Browning, 'he would have finally ranged himself among the Christians': and this notwithstanding the fact that Shelley writes to Horace Smith from Pisa just three months before his death, 'I have not the smallest influence over Lord Byron, and if I had, I certainly should employ it to eradicate from his great mind the delusions of Christianity.' This utterance certainly represents his more obvious and usual attitude: how far it was modified by what Browning felt in him can only be gathered from an examination of his whole attitude toward the orthodox belief of his day. But Shelley's attitude toward Christianity represents one aspect only of his faith, and not the most distinctive or positive aspect. For a full understanding of that faith it becomes necessary to examine also his beliefs regarding the immortality of the soul, the doctrine of necessity, the perfectibility of human nature, and certain other high spiritual conceptions. Though his poetry is the supreme expression of these ideas, and embodies conceptions beyond the possibility of prose, the present writer does not share the view that the bearing of his prose writings on his faith is unimportant, and that light is only to be found in what he wrote by way of ecstasy.   In the present essay his letters and essays have been constantly quoted: yet they have been quoted not for their own sake, but for the light they throw on the central conceptions of his poetry.

I

His attitude toward God and Christianity, like the rest of his beliefs, cannot be understood without a glance at the successive stages of his experience and thought.

As an undergraduate we find him fulminating against orthodoxy and intolerance, yet invoking solemnly, in a letter to Hogg, God, whose 'mercy is great'.. A little later he declares that 'it is impossible not to believe in the soul of the universe, the intelligent and necessarily beneficent actuating principle'.   His proof of this is exactly that of the mystics; he says: 'I may not be able to adduce proofs, but I think that the leaf of a tree, the meanest insect on which we trample, are in themselves arguments more conclusive than any which can be advanced, that some vast intellect animates infinity.' This is nearly Blake's answer:

> He who replies to words of doubt
> Doth put the light of knowledge out.
> A riddle or the cricket's cry
> Is to doubt a fit reply.

I believe that this utterance represents the positive aspect of Shelley's faith, his more profound and characteristic intuition of the universe, and that, despite

seeming inconsistencies and contradictions, it persisted
to the end throughout his poetry and prose, always
flaming forth when his mind was working most fervently
and deeply, and never being totally overwhelmed by the
impulse toward negation and 'rationalism' that was also
in him. It is a noteworthy, yet insufficiently noted, fact
that only two months before he was expelled from
Oxford for circulating *The Necessity of Atheism*, we find
him arguing hotly with Hogg for the existence of
a Deity. 'I here take God (and a God exists) to witness',
he writes. . . .'O, that this Deity were the soul of the
universe, the spirit of universal imperishable love.'
Though drawn to this, as to the lode-star of his faith,
and now, as nearly always, detesting what he calls
'materialism', he will not admit Christianity, and flings
it to the ruthless Hogg to mangle. A little earlier he
had attacked his father's 'equine argument', 'I believe
because I do believe.' So far, it would seem, he had
objected less to faith than to particular forms of it; but
a distinct hardening is noticeable immediately after his
expulsion from Oxford, and it is difficult not to attribute
this directly to the crass injustice—as it seemed to him—
with which he had been used. Love of a Deity, be he
Allah or Brahma, he now says, proceeds from fear:
faith is requisite for the vulgar: the enlightened should
reject it. On the ground of feeling, pure and simple, he
has no objection to a Deity; but he bids Elizabeth
Hitchener dismiss Christianity as 'militating' against
truth and reason. He has now thrown over even
Deism: 'I once was an enthusiastic deist,' he tells
Elizabeth, 'but never a Christian.' Christianity, he
thinks, 'militates with virtue'. There is a curious
forecast of Nietzsche in his mockery of Faber's 'Christian

mildness, his consistent forgiveness of injuries': one is at once reminded of Blake's reference to Antichrist as 'creeping Jesus', who 'would have done anything to please us', and of his claim that

> The Vision of Christ that thou dost see
> Is my vision's greatest enemy.

The Christian Heaven, thinks Shelley, is no Paradise: how could it be when its possessors feel that one-half of their fellow creatures are doomed to eternal destruction? Far better the Iroquois conception of 'human life perfected'. The divinity of Christ is impossible. Before Shelley's expulsion from Oxford he tells us that he had become an atheist; but note the significant qualification, 'in the popular sense of the word God.' The remarks just quoted, nearly all of which are addressed to Elizabeth Hitchener, belong to one year (1811), that which was to witness his expulsion from Oxford. This occurrence, I repeat, is of the utmost significance, and is one of the main causes of the violence characterizing his attacks on the recognized faith, the other cause being the influence of William Godwin, whose *Political Justice* he had already read while at Eton, and who exercised a strong, though not a determining, influence over him for some years afterwards. Godwin had a certain religious sense: but in the Sixth Book of *Political Justice* he attacked much that is ordinarily understood by religion, and in a letter to H. B. Rosser he writes, 'in the vulgar acceptation of the word I think a man is right who does not believe in God.' With Godwin's influence upon Shelley, and its limitations, I shall deal immediately, as with that quite different strain in him which even at this age made him fly from reason to intuition for a vindication of his belief in immortality and elective affinities. At present it may be said that, towards the end of his correspondence with Elizabeth Hitchener, his wrath at his expulsion had cooled, and so already, in some measure, had Godwin's influence. Also, Shelley had eased his mind of much perilous stuff through the publication of *Queen Mab* and its notes. The result is a decrease of violence, though not of conviction, and a decrease, also, throughout his subsequent correspondence, of references to religion. As there is but little change in this particular aspect of his belief and teaching till immediately before his death, we may discuss the matter in its general bearings, and consider the exact meaning and limitation of Shelley's hatred of Christianity. Here two main aspects at once disengage themselves. Two things Shelley hated with the greatest intensity—historical Christianity, or Paulinism, if one likes to call it so, the accretion of dogma and, as he considered it, of blind and wicked misinterpretation, the tradition of cruelty, oppression, and intolerance which, in his opinion, had darkened the light of Christ's teaching, and turned a religion of love into one of hatred and mistrust. This abhorrence was heightened by his reverence for the classical genius which had been thwarted and deadened, in his opinion, by the new faith. Thus he says in *Queen Mab*:

> Where Cicero and Antoninus lived,
> A cowled and hypocritical monk
> Prays, curses and deceives.

Writing to Peacock, he deplores the downfall of Greek culture and civilization, and adds: ' But for the Christian religion, which put the finishing stroke on the ancient system; but for those changes that conducted Athens to its ruin—to what an eminence might not humanity have arrived!' To Godwin he writes: 'The first doubts which arose in my boyish mind concerning the genuineness of the Christian religion, as a revelation from the divinity, were excited by a contemplation of the virtues and genius of Greece and Rome. Shall Socrates and Cicero perish whilst the meanest hind of modern England inherits eternal life?' And towards the end of his life, writing from Pisa to Southey, he says: 'I confess your recommendation to adopt the system of ideas you call Christianity has little weight with me. To judge of the doctrines by their effects, one would think that this religion were called the religion of Christ and Charity "ut lucus a non lucendo", when I consider the manner in which they seem to have transformed the disposition and understanding of you and men of the most amiable manners and the highest accomplishments, so that even when recommending Christianity you cannot forbear breathing out defiance, against the express words of Christ.' In a letter to Leigh Hunt he denies 'that the whole mass of ancient Hebrew literature is of Divine authority', and again, writing to Elizabeth Hitchener, he repudiates the Deity 'who beheld with favour the coward wretch Abraham, who built the grandeur of his favourite Jews on the bleeding bodies of myriads, on the subjugated necks of the dispossessed inhabitants of Canaan.' 'But here', he adds, 'my instances were as long as the memoir of his furious king-like exploits, did not contempt succeed to hatred.' This seems to be an echo of the passage in *Queen Mab* in which he had execrated the time and place where

an inhuman and uncultured race
Howled hideous praises to their Demon-God.

According to Gilfillan and De Quincey, the very mention of Christianity would throw Shelley into a transfiguration, or ecstasy, of hate. Strong contributory causes of his scepticism and anti-Christian feeling are considered by Medwin to have been the removal of his children by that 'priestly pest', the Lord Chancellor, the unfavourable review of *The Revolt of Islam* by a divine, and the persecution of Dr. Nott. Too much may, perhaps, be made of the influence of such external influences as these on Shelley's faith, but they must always be given weight as secondary causes.

Instances of these somewhat obvious aspects of Shelley's teaching might be multiplied indefinitely, as well as of the denial of Christ's divinity expressed in these words to Elizabeth Hitchener: 'You seem much to doubt Christianity; I do not; I cannot conceive in my mind even the possibility of its genuineness. What is now to be thought of Jesus Christ's divinity? To me it appears clear as day that it is the falsehood of human kind.' At one period of his life, too, Shelley, not content with denying Christ's divinity, had even shown signs of doubting His sincerity and beneficence. In *Queen Mab*, Ahasuerus, who had been the hero of a still earlier poem, indicts Christ as 'a malignant soul' who, under the pretence of bringing peace, truth and justice to earth, lights men's souls with 'quenchless flames of zeal' and strife. In the notes to the same poem Shelley discounts the homage he pays to Christ the Man—as opposed to the traditionary Christ of Ahasuerus' account —by adding in a footnote: 'Since writing this note I have some reason to suspect that Jesus was an ambitious man who aspired to the throne of Judaea.'

It is perhaps hardly profitable to discuss in close detail

the crude and youthful poem which Shelley afterwards repudiated: I ónly do so in order to emphasize the marked change in his attitude toward Christ, and the ever-increasing sympathy and reverence for His personality, which are evident in his later writings. This change is already noticeable in the *Address to the Irish People*, and the *Proposal for an Association of Philanthropists* (both 1812), both of which contain appeals to the example of Jesus; and it is still more strikingly evident in *Prometheus* (Act I, 1. 546), where Christ is shown weeping over Christianity:

> One came forth of gentle worth
> Smiling on the sanguine earth;
> His words outlived him, like swift poison
>   Withering up truth, peace, and pity.
> Look! where round the wide horizon
>   Many a million-peopled city
> Vomits smoke in the bright air.
> Hark that outcry of despair!
> 'Tis his mild and gentle ghost
>   Wailing for the faith he kindled:
> Look again, the flames almost
>   To a glow-worm's lamp have dwindled.

Similarly, in one of the fragments connected with *Epipsychidion* he says:

> And Socrates, the Jesus Christ of Greece,
> And Jesus Christ Himself, did never cease
> To urge all living things to love each other,
> And to forgive their mutual faults, and smother
> The Devil of disunion in their souls.

But by far the most important and striking tribute to Christ is paid in *Hellas*, written only a few months before Shelley's death. Throughout this dramatic poem the Cross is taken as the symbol of beneficence and regeneration, as opposed to the Crescent, and Christ is the Promethean conqueror:

A power from the unknown God,
  A Promethean conqueror, came;
Like a triumphal path he trod
  The thorns of death and shame.
A mortal shape to him
Was like the vapour dim
Which the orient planet animates with light;
  Hell, Sin, and Slavery came,
  Like bloodhounds mild and tame,
Nor preyed, until their Lord had taken flight;
  The moon of Mahomet
  Arose, and it shall set:
While blazoned as on Heaven's immortal noon
  The cross leads generations on.

This passage is at once amplified and limited by
Shelley's note: 'The popular notions of Christianity
are represented in this chorus as true in their relation to
the worship they superseded, and that which in all
probability they will supersede, without considering
their merits in a relation more universal.'

Here we have a very different utterance from that
which condemns Christianity utterly as the mean and
barbarous faith which dealt its death-blow to the older
culture: and one certainly seems to see indications that if
Shelley had lived to consider the merits of Christianity
'in a more universal relation', he would have shown an
even deeper admiration for the spirit underlying it.
Indeed, in Christ's own speech in the Prologue to *Hellas*
—which has no note to limit it, and clearly represents
Shelley's own view of Christ—Christianity in its original
form is represented as the complement and crown of the
Grecian spirit, Christ being preferred even to Plato,
usually the idol of Shelley's worship:

          —by Plato's sacred light,
  Of which my spirit was a burning morrow—
  By Greece and all she cannot cease to be,

> Her quenchless words, sparks of immortal truth,
> Stars of all night—her harmonies and forms,
> Echoes and shadows of what love adores
> In thee, I do compel thee, send forth Fate,
> Thy irrevocable child: let her descend,
> A seraph-wingéd Victory arrayed
> In tempest of the omnipotence of God
> Which sweeps through all things.

More will be said of *Hellas* towards the end of this essay.

II

It is obvious, however, that a man might have a profound reverence for the personality of Christ, and yet find his account in rationalism and even atheism. Are we to believe that the title of Atheist, by which he was known at Eton, and his signature, ἄθεος, in a Swiss hotel book, represent Shelley's final religious position? Here again we must examine the evidence in detail, and in the light of what we know of the evolution of his mind. His youthful fluctuations of opinion concerning the Deity have already been described; but, as his life proceeds, the issue becomes wider and more complicated. His whole physical history, from his boyhood onwards, resolves itself into a conflict between the rationalizing habit which had been developed in him through the influence of certain of his contemporaries, and the mystical impulse of his inmost nature. His letters to Elizabeth Hitchener—our most important documents as to his faith at this period—are full of inconsistencies. On the one hand he declares that reason is his substitute for God, and he objects to Christianity that it does not admit of argument, and is based merely on passion. The term God is thus only acceptable if it is made synonymous with morality, which does satisfy reason. Shelley quotes with approval Helvétius' statement that 'Morality is accordant, universal and uniform, therefore it is the Work of God'. Religion in any other sense is immoral and positively bad for man. 'God is an hypothesis,' he says in the notes to *Queen Mab*, 'and as such stands in need of proof: the *onus probandi* rests on the Theist.' Many more instances of the same belief might be advanced; but those just quoted supply a fairly clear portrait of Shelley the sceptic and rationalist. Yet side by side with him, and penning in the very same letter convictions the opposite of his, is Shelley the Platonist and mystic.

Nowhere does this aspect of Shelley's faith emerge more constantly or strikingly than when he is discussing the immortality of the soul, to the belief in which he clung tenaciously even at the most rationalistic moments of his life. This belief, Shelley tells us in his *Essay on a Future State*, is totally foreign to the question of God's existence, and to that of future rewards and punishments. Sometimes he attempts a logical proof of it through arguments now Platonic, now scientific. Writing to Elizabeth Hitchener (June 20, 1811) he uses the arguments of the conservation of energy and the imperishability of matter to prove that 'neither will soul perish; that in a future existence it will lose all consciousness of having formerly lived elsewhere—will begin life anew, possibly under a shape of which we have now no idea. But we have no right to make hypotheses —this is not one: at least I flatter myself that I have kept clear of supposition.' Again (June 25, 1811) he points to the suspension of the soul's waking faculties during sleep, and argues for a similar suspension in

Death. But his most remarkable utterance on this subject, and the one which illustrates most strikingly the dual nature of his mind, is that in which he throws over reason as his guide in this matter, and falls back on that inward sense which gives her the lie direct (October 10, 1811): 'Certainly reason can never either account for, or prove the truth of, feeling. I have considered it in every possible light, and reason tells me that death is the boundary of the life of man, and yet I feel, I believe, the direct contrary. The senses are the only inlets of knowledge, and there is an inward sense that has persuaded me of this.' In a succeeding letter (November 24, 1811) he agrees with Miss Hitchener that 'this imagination' (i.e. the 'inward sense' just referred to) is a proof of the soul's immortality, and he claims that even flowers have souls, and offers a teleological explanation of their existence. Also, having previously hailed Miss Hitchener as the 'sister of his soul', he propounds a highly transcendental theory of elective affinities. Later, he tells us 'the creation of the soul at birth is a thing I do not like',[1] and again he assures Elizabeth that he does not doubt the eternity of the soul.[2] In his early poem *The Retrospect* he says:

> And early I had learned to scorn
> The chains of clay that bound a soul
> Panting to seize the wings of morn.

It should be noted that these passages are written during the most fiercely rationalistic crisis of Shelley's life— that in which he attacks virtually every conception of divinity as incompatible with finite reason.

As early as 1812 he had had some conversation with

---

[1] Ingpen's edition of Shelley's letters, vol. i, p. 78.
[2] Ingpen, vol. i, p. 217.

Southey, which, so he tells us, elicited his own true opinions of God : and Southey, detecting the incongruity between his beliefs and his professions, had told him that he ought not to call himself an atheist, since in reality he believed that the universe was God. He was, in fact, said Southey, a pantheist. This pantheism is fairly well marked in *Queen Mab*, in one passage of which the Spirit of Nature is invoked as the Soul of the smallest being as of 'those mighty spheres whose changeless paths through Heaven's deep silence lie'. Here man, like external nature, unconsciously fulfils the will of the spirit, and works forward at her behest to the reign of endless peace. This Spirit, it must be noted, is at the present stage something external to human mind and sense ; so that, at this period, there is a fundamental difference between Shelley's impelling Spirit and that of Wordsworth,

> Whose dwelling is the light of setting suns
> And the round ocean and the living air,
> And the blue sky, and in the mind of man.

III

Shelley's conception of the nature of this spirit is closely related to his conception of Necessity—or rather, to the conception which at this period he was willing to take over from William Godwin, but which he modified throughout the course of his later writings till it passed into a quite different belief. The doctrine is developed in *Political Justice* in relation both to the Universe and to the individual human life, concerning which Godwin writes : ' He who affirms that all actions are necessary means that if we form a just and complete view of all the circumstances in which a living or intelligent being is

placed, we shall find that he could not in any moment
of his existence have acted otherwise than he has acted.'
Later we shall discuss this doctrine in relation to
Godwin's general philosophy: here, it is important to
notice that at the period of *Queen Mab*, when Shelley
still subscribed to the Godwinian necessitarianism, his
universal spirit is quite definitely Necessity itself:

> Even the minutest molecule of light,
> That in an April sunbeam's fleeting glow
> Fulfils its destined though invisible work,
> The universal Spirit guides.

And again he writes:

> Spirit of Nature! all-sufficing Power,
> Necessity! thou mother of the world![1]

In a long note on *Queen Mab*[2] (vi. 198), he gives Necessity
authority over Mind no less than Matter, and says that
it ' utterly destroys religion '.   This note is full of youth-

---

[1] Cf. his note to *Queen Mab*, i. 252-3: ' Millions and millions
of suns are ranged around us, all attended by innumerable worlds,
yet calm, regular and harmonious, all keeping the paths of
immutable necessity.'

[2] It is almost impossible to reconcile the speculations regarding
Nature embodied in this poem.   In vi. 157 we find her working
impartially for good and for evil.   She 'strengthens in health and
poisons in disease'.   She resembles the stuff of which the world,
according to Arnold's *Empedocles*, is spun :

> That we who rail are still,
> With what we rail at, one;
> One with the o'erlaboured Power that through the breadth
> and length
>
> Of earth, and air, and sea,
> In men, and plants, and stones,
> Hath toil perpetually,
> And travails, pants and moans;
> Fain would do all things well, but sometimes fails in strength.

But in vi. 54-7 she works consciously toward perfection, and with
recreating hand will soon blot ' the blood-stained charter of all woe
in mercy from the book of Earth '.

ful fallacies and is really an unconscious argument for determinism, and the uniformity of Nature : but it at least avoids the arch-fallacy by which Godwin tried to combine Necessitarianism with the doctrine of a purposive progress toward human perfection.   In a note on the famous pronouncement, ' There is no God ' (vii. 13), Shelley draws a distinction of considerable significance for the comprehension of his position, and the dualism of thought which underlies it.   The negation, he says, must be understood solely to affect a *creative* deity.   The hypothesis of a pervading spirit coeternal with the universe remains unshaken.   His belief in this pervading spirit henceforth remains with him till the end : but his conception of its nature is modified in most noteworthy respects.

If in his conception of the universal spirit, as declared in this poem, Shelley attempts, somewhat vainly, to reconcile Godwinism with Platonism, in his conception of the soul, here as elsewhere, the Platonic intuition predominates.   Soul is the only element throughout the world : she is pure in her nature, and, though soiled by earth, is still capable of regaining her original perfection :

Soul is not more polluted than the beams
Of Heaven's pure orb, ere round their rapid lines
The taint of earth-born atmospheres arise.

Here Shelley's utterance is almost that of the stanzas of *Nosce Teipsum* in which Sir John Davies likens the soul to the morning light :

Abiding pure, when the air is most corrupted ;
Throughout the air her beams dispersing wide,
And when the air is tost, not interrupted :

So doth the piercing Soul the body fill
Being all in all.

There is a Wordsworthian note in Shelley's reference
to 'that strange state before the naked soul has found
its home'.

Towards the end of *Queen Mab*, and of its 'revised
version', *The Daemon of the World*, the transcendental
impulse has found greater depth and strength. Mind
is universal and omnipotent, life being the mere material
means through which it realizes itself in the world of
phenomena :

> For birth but wakes the universal mind
> Whose mighty streams might else in silence flow
> Thro' the vast world, to individual sense
> Of outward shows, whose unexperienced shape
> New modes of passion to its frame may lend;
> Life is its state of action.

At the beginning of *Alastor* the same thought runs, in
a form less expository than before, and far more sensuous
and beautiful.   One passage has almost the thought and
cadence of *Tintern Abbey*, though it is significant of
Shelley's whole nature and genius that he reaches
universal spirit, not through Nature watched and wooed
in the simpler and more elemental aspects known to
Wordsworth, but through the weird midnight com-
munings of his soul with her, through incommunicable
dream, through twilight phantasms and deep noonday
thought, till he can say :

> serenely now
> And moveless, as a long-forgotten lyre
> Suspended in the solitary dome
> Of some mysterious and deserted fane,
> I wait thy breath, Great Parent, that my strain
> May modulate with murmurs of the air,
> And motions of the forests and the sea,
> And voice of living beings, and woven hymns
> Of night and day, and the deep heart of man.

In his divided allegiance to Nature and to his own imagination, Shelley, here, as often, is midway between Wordsworth, who saw all things, man, God, and his own soul, through Nature's teaching, and Blake, who turned back for inspiration to the imaginings of his own soul and wrote 'natural objects always did, and do now, weaken, deaden and obliterate imagination in me. Wordsworth must know that what he writes valuable is not to be found in Nature.'

The sequence of Shelley's poems, then, in so far as these discuss the nature of the universe, shows a distinct deepening of thought and a growing transcendentalism of outlook. For our present purpose it becomes especially important to note the gradual steps by which he struggled free from the strangling doctrine of determinism. In *Queen Mab*, as we have seen, the Universal Spirit is Necessity, aloof, indifferent, and blind: in certain passages of *The Revolt of Islam* this conception is repeated:

Alas, our thoughts flow on with stream, whose waters
Return not to their fountain—Earth and Heaven,
The Ocean and the Sun, the Clouds their daughters,
Winter, and Spring, and Morn, and Noon, and Even,
All that we are or know, is darkly driven
Towards one gulf.

But elsewhere in the same poem there is an indication that the world-force is beneficent, and strives toward perfection:

Our many thoughts and deeds, our life and love,
Our happiness, and all that we have been,
Immortally must live, and burn and move,
When we shall be no more.

Even in this poem Shelley had seen, as Godwin had never seen, the inconsistency of attempting to realize universal benevolence beneath the sway of a power determined after this fashion: and he had been consequently driven into the Manicheism which recognized good and evil as the two primary and hostile principles embodied respectively in the snake and the eagle. Already in *Julian and Maddalo* the human will is regarded as free:

> it is our will
> That thus enchains us to permitted ill.
> We might be otherwise—we might be all
> We dream of, happy, high, majestical.

In the *Prometheus Unbound* Shelley takes a further step, and dissociates Love, and Love alone, from determinism, from the sway of ' Fate, Time, Occasion, Chance and Change '. In *Adonais* Love is not merely exempt from the sway of such a force, but has actually superseded it, and has itself become the moving spirit of existence:

> That Light whose smile kindles the Universe,
> That Beauty in which all things work and move,
> That Benediction which the eclipsing Curse
> Of birth can quench not, that sustaining Love
> Which through the web of being blindly wove
> By man and beast and earth and air and sea,
> Burns bright or dim, as each are mirrors of
> The fire for which all thirst. [1]

---

[1] It is worth noting that this stanza, which glorifies Love as the universal spirit, had been anticipated in some of Shelley's early and uninspired verse. Thus, in *A Dialogue* (1809) Death speaks:

> Nought waits for the good but a spirit of Love,
> That will hail their blest advent to regions above.
> For Love, Mortal, gleams through the gloom of my sway,
> And the shades which surround me fly fast at its ray.

Similarly in *To Death* (1810) Love is the sole thing exempted from the hand of the Destroyer. *Queen Mab* and the succeeding poems seem to represent a certain interruption of this thought, and an intermediate stage during which, as Mary Shelley tells us, her

If previous writers had ever really imbued Shelley with what he himself describes as 'materialism', he was able to shake off the spell, speedily and for good. According to Medwin he contended that 'no man who had reflected could be a materialist long': later he declares that the doctrines of the French and material philosophy 'are as false as they are pernicious'. In his Essay *On Life* he subscribes to the doctrine that 'nothing exists but as it is perceived': but he is as far from giving this principle a materialistic application as was Berkeley, who had previously formulated it. 'This materialism', he says, 'is a seducing system to young and superficial minds. It allows its disciples to talk, and dispenses them from thinking.' And he continues in words which go to the very heart of his thought : 'but I was discontented with such a view of things as it [materialism] afforded ; man is a being of high aspirations, "looking both before and after," whose "thoughts wander through eternity", disclaiming alliance with transience and decay; incapable of imagining to himself annihilation ; existing but in the future and the past ; being not what he is, but what he has been and shall be. Whatever may be his true and final destination, there is a spirit within him at enmity with nothingness and dissolution. This is the character of all life and being. Each is at once the centre and the circumference ; the point to which all things are referred, and the line in which all things are contained.'[1]

husband had become a temporary convert to French philosophy— and, she might have added, a partial convert to the philosophy of her own father.

[1] Shelley's *Essay on a Future State* deals with the belief in immortality in a way hardly consistent with this passage, and wholly inconsistent with the greater part of his later poetry.

Such a conception, he continues, is equally far removed from materialism on the one hand, and on the other from 'the popular philosophy of mind and matter', with its corollary of the popular God. Shelley's own belief, so he tells us, is in harmony with 'the intellectual philosophy' of Sir William Drummond. Its main tenet is that of unity. The difference between ideas and external objects is merely nominal. Similarly, 'the existence of distinct individual minds, similar to that which is employed in now questioning its own nature; is likewise found to be a delusion. The words *I, you, they*, are not signs of any actual difference subsisting between the assemblage of thoughts thus indicated, but are merely marks employed to denote the different modifications of the one mind.' Here we reach by the road of prose a conception akin to certain main conceptions of Shelley's poetry.

IV

One mind, one power, one all-pervasive spirit, that is after all the cardinal principle of Shelley's philosophy and faith. Like his beloved Plato, he believed that the World possessed a Soul. God, he says to Hogg, is to be erased in favour of the Soul of the Universe, 'the intelligent and necessarily beneficent actuating principle.' This, he says, it is impossible not to believe in. It is difficult, too, to read this part of his work without feeling that it owes much to Spinoza, whom he had read closely and eagerly. Spinoza's conception of Substance is evident in Shelley's conception of a Spirit

---

Students of his work are constantly confronted with discrepancies of this kind. Here we can only state what seems to be his deeper and more positive and consistent view of the matter.

which is the internal, and not the external, cause of all
things, and, conversely, of a nature which is not the
dead sum of things (*natura naturata*), miraculously
manipulated from without, but the vital energizing
spirit inherent in all phenomena (*natura naturans*).
Shelley goes beyond Spinoza, however, in the conception
which recurs throughout his prose, that the First Cause
is a thing wholly different from Mind.   Such a cause as
this he recognizes in numerous passages,—for example,
in his essay *On a Future State*, where he refers to 'that
mysterious principle which regulates the proceedings of
the Universe'; but in his essay *On Life* he declares that
'it is infinitely improbable that the cause of mind—that
is, of existence—is similar to mind', and he says again,
'Mind cannot create: it can only perceive. '

Spinoza had denied that the human attribute of
understanding could be predicated of God, and had
intended this denial as a proof of God's absolute perfection; but Shelley, eager now as always to dissociate
the existence of inward spirit, which he affirmed, from
the principle of external creation, which he frequently,
though by no means always, denied, was at pains to show
that that principle was infinitely remote from so intelligible and necessary a conception as that of human or
cosmic mind.   Hence it is that he says in *The Revolt of
Islam* :

What is that Power? Ye mock yourselves, and give
  A human heart to what ye cannot know:
As if the cause of life could think and live!
  'Twere as if man's own works should feel and show
  The hopes, and fears, and thoughts from which they
    flow,
And he be like to them!

'Mind', he says elsewhere, 'cannot be considered pure.'

And here again we seem to catch an echo of the Spinozan doctrine that Substance (or God) can only enter experience in its Modes (phenomena) and through its Attributes.

It is unfair, however, to judge Shelley, or any other worker through inspiration, only or mainly by his logical processes, however explicitly they may be developed in certain portions of his work. He himself has, in fact, implicitly warned us against this habit in his *Defence of Poetry*. Consequently, though he tells us in his *Speculations on Metaphysics*, that we ought to consider the mind of man and the universe as the great whole on which to exercise our speculations, we prefer to put aside speculations for the nonce, and to meet the same truth *sub specie aeternitatis—et pulchritudinis*—in the great opening of *Mont Blanc*:

The everlasting universe of things
Flows through the mind, and rolls its rapid waves,
Now dark—now glittering—now reflecting gloom—
Now lending splendour, where from secret springs
The source of human thought its tribute brings
Of waters,—with a sound but half its own,
Such as a feeble brook will oft assume
In the wild woods, among the mountains lone,
Where waterfalls around it leap for ever,
Where woods and winds contend, and a vast river
Over its rocks ceaselessly bursts and raves.

The struggle between the transcendental instinct of Shelley's genius, and its rationalistic Godwinian accretions, is again strikingly evident in his *Speculations on Morals*. 'It is admitted', he says, 'that a virtuous or moral action is that action which, when considered in all its accessories and consequences, is fitted to produce the highest pleasure to the greatest number of sensitive beings'; and again he declares 'Virtue is entirely a refinement of civilized life, a creation of the human mind '. These statements, however, must not be taken as supporting any narrowly utilitarian view of ethics. Benevolence in its true form was to Shelley 'disinterested', and the result of a cultivated *imagination*, displayed towards the suffering of others. He was clearly drawn in some sense towards the utilitarian position through his sympathy with its antagonism towards dogmatic Christianity : but the opposite impulse of his soul is evident in his contention that 'Justice and benevolence result from the elementary laws of the human mind', that 'the internal influence, derived from the constitution of the mind from which they flow, produces that peculiar modification of actions which makes them intrinsically good or evil', and that 'according to the elementary principles of the mind, man is capable of desiring and pursuing good for its own sake'. Here we are far nearer to the Categorical Imperative, the eternal voice within demanding man's unconditional allegiance, than we are to rationalistic logic or utilitarianism : but the Categorical Imperative, or rather the relationship of moral virtue to happiness as conceived by Kant,[1] leads him to postulate

---

[1] It is curious that Shelley, with his love and knowledge of Plato, should have been rather repelled than attracted by the great modern continuer of the Platonic tradition. In *Peter Bell the Third* he refers to 'Kant's book' as

> A world of words, tail foremost, where
> Right—wrong—false—true—and foul—and fair,
> As in a lottery-wheel are shook.

He possessed a large edition of Kant, but it was Hogg's belief that he had never read it. Writing to Claire Clairmont of German philosophy in general, he says, 'As far as I can understand it it contemplates only the silver side of the shield of truth : better in this respect than the French, who only saw the narrow edge of it.' (*Letters*, p. 853.)

the agency of a God or Supreme Reason transcending
the nature of man; and in this particular relation,
Shelley never explicitly admits the operation of such a
power. Yet it is not necessary to conclude from these
passages that he has fallen into any inconsistency when
he makes Virtue at once an *a priori* law and a secondary
product. It is both of these things, he might have said,
according as it is considered in its essence or its content.
With Plato, the Idea of the Good was banished from man's
consciousness at birth, and only returned to it through
that turning of the soul to the light which is the true
education : hence Virtue with him, though intuitive, was
realizable only with difficulty, through recollection, or
the recapturing of the Idea of the Good by the human
soul. We may well believe that in the above passages,
as elsewhere, Shelley was consciously or unconsciously
influenced by Plato, and may therefore conclude that
Plato's teaching regarding the dual nature of Virtue
was accepted by Shelley and made his own.

V

To Aristotle morality was essentially the formed habit :
with Kant, on the other hand, the moral essential was
the *effort* after virtue, the struggle and victory being the
ultimate criterion. To Shelley, however, Virtue in its
highest form of self-sacrifice was neither a habit nor an
effort, but a passion, an instinctive and ecstatic affirmation of the universal principle of Love, in which all
beauty, thought, prudence, virtue, and poetry were
combined and transfigured. This unity is well brought
out in the chorus of Beneficent Spirits of the First Act
of *Prometheus.* Here the First Spirit represents spiritual
enlightenment, the Third that passion for learning which

Plato had called the intellectual Eros, and considered
akin to sexual passion in its most pure and spiritual
form. The Fourth Spirit represents passion working
beneath the law of beauty, and finding its own words
and music in the highest and most conscious form of
art. It is the spirit inspiring the poet who

> will watch from dawn to gloom
> The lake-reflected sun illume
> The yellow bees in the ivy-bloom,
> Nor heed nor see, what things they be;
> But from these create he can
> Forms more real than living man,
> Nurslings of immortality!

The Second Spirit is the highest passion of the soul,
love of one's kind, losing and finding itself in death
undergone for their sake :

> I heard the thunder hoarsely laugh:
> Mighty fleets were strewn like chaff
> And spread beneath a hell of death
> O'er the white waters. I alit
> On a great ship lightning-split,
> And speeded hither on the sigh
> Of one who gave an enemy
> His plank, then plunged aside to die.

This passage illustrates at once Shelley's conception of
Virtue and its relation to other forms of truth and
beauty, and it is also inspired with that craving for unity
which has been shown by a great living critic to be one
of the master-passions of his soul. It illustrates that
intense feeling for the beauty of ethical goodness which
recurs constantly throughout his poetry and puts him in
touch with the Cambridge Platonists.

Wordsworth had a far more catholic and minute sense
than had Shelley of such beauty in its spiritual aspects,
and after his emancipation from the Godwinian worship

of 'reason', he deliberately sought it in the humble and unsophisticated types of humankind. Also, he some-times deliberately subordinated sensuous beauty to spiritual, for the spirit's exaltation. But Shelley knew no such divorce. Though his love of mankind in the mass was more intense than Wordsworth's, he had far less understanding than he of the lowly men and women who compose it. On the other hand, he had certainly more passion than Wordsworth. For both these causes he knew no

> dim recollections
> Of pedlars tramping on their rounds;
> Milk-pans and pails; and odd collections
> Of saws, and proverbs; and reflections
> Old parsons make in burying-grounds.

It was largely through his antipathy to these things, and his conviction of Wordsworth's preoccupation with them, that he came to consider the poet of *Tintern Abbey* as

> a kind of moral eunuch,
> He touched the hem of Nature's shift,
> Felt faint—and never dared uplift
> The closest, all-concealing tunic.

Certain it is that with Shelley, owing at once to his more ardent nature and to his instinct for unity, goodness is ever near to sensuous beauty, and passes easily into passion. Hence his choice of heroic types rather than simple ones, of Laon, Cythna, and Prometheus rather than Michael, Matthew, and the Leechgatherer. Laon and Cythna possess youth and strength and beauty, no less than courage and the instinct for self-sacrifice, and their passion for free-dom, as described in Canto V of *The Revolt of Islam*, shifts swiftly into the amorous passion of Canto VI. Prometheus is not merely a deliverer, but a lover and

a poet. A further admirable instance of this harmony
of goodness and beauty is seen in the description of
the Lady Beneficent who tended the garden of 'the
Sensitive Plant':

A Lady, the wonder of her kind,
Whose form was upborne by a lovely mind
Which, dilating, had moulded her mien and motion
Like a sea-flower unfolded beneath the ocean,

Tended the garden from morn to even:
And the meteors of that sublunar Heaven,
Like the lamps of the air when Night walks forth,
Laughed round her footsteps up from the Earth!

She had no companion of mortal race,
But her tremulous breath and her flushing face
Told, whilst the morn kissed the sleep from her eyes,
That her dreams were less slumber than Paradise.

Similarly, in the *Ode to Naples* the Spirit of Love and
Beneficence shines lovely in her star 'o'er Ocean's
western floor', and is the

Spirit of beauty! at whose soft command
The sunbeams and the showers distil its foison
From the Earth's bosom chill.

With many writers this association would represent
the mere artist's instinct, that morality to become poetic-
ally tolerable must first be brought beneath the law
of beauty; but this instinct, though strong in Shelley,
was largely unconscious, and his lapses from it drew
down upon him the admonition of Keats, that he should
'curb his magnanimity and be more of an artist'. Both
the association and the instinct, indeed, have with him
their origin in something far deeper, and take us to the
very heart of his faith. In his *Defence of Poetry* he tells
us that a poet participates in the eternal, the infinite,
and the one, and that a poem is the very image of life

expressed in its eternal truth. It is the 'creation of actions according to the unchangeable forms of human nature, *as existing in the mind of the Creator*, which is itself the image of all other minds'. Plato had described the poet as an imitator removed in the third degree from ideal truth and beauty. To Shelley, on the other hand, he was not so removed, but was at their very heart. He partook of that ideal genius of which virtue, truth, and beauty were the indissociable kinds, and therefore his portrayal of any one of these must needs be suffused with the glory of the others. Hence he was, in the fullest sense of the word, a creator—*non merita nome di creatore se non Iddio ed il Poeta,*—and a creator does not preach, but makes. And as beauty and love were the creative laws of life, so too they became the creative laws of art, unconsciously, inevitably, and not through any studied device of technical refinement. Conversely, didacticism is excluded from the highest poetry, for didacticism deals with the transitory, art at its highest with the eternal. And here we come upon certain passages which show us how utterly mistaken is the theory lately propounded which regards Shelley as the mere sequel of Godwin,[1] and of the other writers of the day, French and English, who strove to reduce life to

[1] Who writes thus: 'Justice, as it was defined in a previous chapter, is coincident with utility. I am myself a part of the great whole, and my happiness is part of that complex view of things by which justice is regulated.' (*Political Justice*, Book II, chap. 6.)

'The criterion of morals is utility.' (*Ibidem*, Book VIII, chap. 2.)

'The doctrine of necessity being admitted, it follows that the theory of the human mind is properly, like the theory of every other series of events with which we are acquainted, a system of mechanism, understanding by mechanism nothing more than a regular connection of phenomena without any uncertainty of event.' (*Ibidem*, Book IV, chap. 9.)

a mechanical or utilitarian pattern, and cramp it in the vice of finite 'reason'. To the noble moral purpose of such men as these, and to their iconoclastic prowess, Shelley here, as always, renders hearty tribute; but he continues: 'Undoubtedly the promoters of utility, in this limited sense, have their appointed office in society. They follow the footsteps of poets, and copy the sketches of their creations into the book of common life. Their exertions are of the highest value, so long as they confine their administration of the concerns of the inferior powers of our nature within the limits due to the superior ones. But while the sceptic destroys gross superstitions, let him spare to deface, as some of the French writers have defaced, the eternal truths charactered upon the imaginations of men.' Similarly, while declaring that the exertions of Locke, Hume, Gibbon, Voltaire, Rousseau, and their disciples, in favour of oppressed and deluded humanity, are entitled to the gratitude of mankind, Shelley declares that, had they never existed, 'a little more nonsense would have been talked for a century or two,' and that there the matter would have ceased: whereas it is impossible to conceive what would have been the condition of the world had Dante, Shakespeare, Milton, and other great poets never existed. Their influence makes for good by working on the imagination, and is of the utmost moral import, precisely because it does not preach morality. The greatest poetry quickens all life at its very source: it 'redeems from decay the visitations of the divinity in man'.

The Defence of Poetry supplies the best possible illustration of the growing transcendentalism of Shelley's mind.

VI

Shelley's abandonment of the doctrine of Necessity, and his insistence on the universal regenerative power of Love, are closely bound up with his conception of human perfectibility.   It is impossible to see whence he derived this conception, or what he meant by it, without a glance at its previous history.   Although the belief in perfectibility was quickened all over Europe by the theories implicit in the French Revolution, it has its basis much farther back in the history of European thought. During the later part of the seventeenth century and the earlier part of the eighteenth, 'common-sense' philosophy, revolting against the romantic exuberance of the pre-ceding age, had tended to regard nature as a wild yet finite growth which would eventually be tamed and trimmed into ordered uniformity by the civilizing hand of man.   Reason was the supreme arbiter—reason which curbed and disciplined the spirit of man, rather than imagination, which spurred it towards and over the limits of reality.   At first this impulse was applied to conservative ends, and in England the aspiration towards cosmic order and finality was set to reinforce the political order and security which had come into the country with the Revolution of 1688.   The conception of Locke, that all ideas proceed from experience, had helped to create the opinion that all the essential data of enlightenment and the new order were now before man, and that his only task was one of combination and construction.   But as the century wore on and certain limitations of this belief became apparent, the old reactionary ideas received a progressive and eventually a revolutionary bias. Just as the conception of the social contract advanced in favour of monarchical control by Hobbes. was wrested towards individual freedom and the general will by Rousseau, so the conception of perfectibility was taken over by the forerunners of the French Revolution, and theoretically based upon a new social order which should arise, not through the development of the old order, but through its destruction. The conception took opposite forms in different writers. Holbach and La Mettrie expressly denied the spiritual element in the universe, and thus partly justified Shelley's sweeping association of French philosophy with materialism. Diderot, on the other hand, thought no less nobly of the soul than did Malvolio, and denied, in express antagonism to the writers just mentioned, that the psychical processes can be explained merely as an interaction of material elements. Helvétius had inculcated closer union between the individual and a reconstructed state, and had based the possibility of such union on an enlightened self-interest, inculcated through an improved system of education. Rousseau, attracted by the converse view of the matter, regarded, not self-interest, but feeling, as the motive force of human progress, and asserted, against the cramping civilization of his day, the indefeasible right of the human soul to develop, through Nature, that single law of its being whose service is perfect freedom. Afterwards a kindred conception of individual right was to be given a more practical and political bias by Thomas Paine, and was to mould the destinies of the two greatest among modern republics. Implicit in all these thinkers, and explicit in many of them, was the conception that no limit could

be set to human progress, and that, once the new order
had displaced the old, man would be led on to

Ambrosial heights of possible acquist
Where souls of men with soul of man consort,
And all look higher to new loveliness
Begotten of the look.

The most eloquent utterance of this faith is that of
Condorcet, who on the eve of his death declared his
belief in an ultimate perfectibility of man, based on
perfect equality, the union of the civic and the individual
conscience, and a universal brotherhood inspired and
safeguarded alike by feeling and by reason.   Europe was
alive with the certainty of universal regeneration.   'Bliss
was it in that dawn to be alive, but to be young was
very heaven.'   It was at this time that Wordsworth,
visiting France, came beneath the sway of that noble
soldier, Michel Beaupuys, and felt with him

That a benignant spirit was abroad
Which might not be withstood, that poverty
Abject as this would in a little time
Be found no more, that we should see the earth
Unthwarted in her wish to recompense
The meek, the lowly, patient child of toil,
All institutes for ever blotted out
That legalized exclusion, empty pomp
Abolished, sensual state and cruel power
Whether by edict of the one or few.

It was now, too, that Coleridge and Southey could
contemplate leaving England, to realize on the banks of
the Susquehannah their scheme—according to Byron,
'less moral than 'twas clever'—of communistic Panti-
socracy; and it was now, too, that William Godwin,
inspired by the spirit of the age, wrote the work which,
according to Hazlitt, became at once 'a standard in the
history of letters'.

If a book could be judged by the effect it exercised on contemporary men of genius, one would be forced to accept this verdict upon the *Enquiry concerning Political Justice*. Godwin quickened, though he did not kindle, the enthusiasm for 'reason' which caught Wordsworth during his earlier manhood, and led him for a while to unsoul

> by syllogistic words
> Those mysteries of being which have made,
> And shall continue evermore to make,
> Of the whole human race one brotherhood.

He determined, for a while, the aspirations of Coleridge, fanned Southey's short-lived radicalism, launched Bulwer upon literature, and won the affectionate regard of Charles Lamb. His influence on Shelley was definite and obvious, though it has lately been considerably exaggerated. Godwin's philosophy was first and foremost ethical and sociological. Entering on the realm of metaphysics, it had no sound metaphysical basis, is therefore full of logical fallacies, and is to-day of little interest or worth, save to the curious student. Keenly alive to the evil in life as he sees it at his day, Godwin starts by inquiring whether this is due to nature or to civilization, and he decides at once against the latter. Men are not bad or miserable by nature: they are made so by the pressure of external circumstance. Their natural inequalities are almost negligible: the main differences between them are due to their education and environment.[1] Man, moreover, belongs to

---

[1] 'I shall attempt to prove two things—first, that the actions and dispositions of mankind are the offspring of circumstances, and not of any original determination that they bring into the world ; and, secondly, that the great stream of our voluntary actions essentially

a universe subject to the law of necessity,[1] and it follows
from this that if the total sum of external things affecting
him can be changed, there will be a corresponding
change, operating with rigorous mathematical certainty,[2]
in his character and soul.   Hence, if perfection of
environment could once be realized, man would
automatically become perfect too.   In his struggle for
perfection, then, his opponent is not a primary law
of nature, human or cosmic, but a secondary condition
of circumstance, which, however cruel and hideous and
invincible it may seem, is ultimately alterable at his will.
To progress toward perfection, he has only to follow
humbly and faithfully that Reason which is at once the
basis of his volition and the cure for all human evil and
suffering.   In the ethical sphere reason will prompt him
to act for the benefit of the whole community ; but that
benefit will be obtained not through obedience to creeds
and governments, but through their destruction,[3] and the

depends, not upon the direct and immediate impulses of sense,
but upon the decisions of the understanding.'

'The essential differences that are to be found between
individual and individual originate in the opinions they form and
the circumstances by which they are controlled.'

'The characters of men are determined in all their most essential circumstances by education'—education being described as
including accident, precept, and political institution. (*Political
Justice*, Book I, chap. 5.)

'The principles of justice, as explained in the preceding chapter,
proceed upon the assumption of the equality of mankind.' (*Ibidem*,
Book II, chap. 3.)

[1] See the quotation from *Political Justice* given on p. 21.

[2] See the third paragraph of footnote on p. 36.

[3] 'With what delight must every well-informed friend of mankind
look forward to the auspicious period, the dissolution of political
government, of that brute engine which has been the only
perennial cause of the vices of mankind, and which, as has
abundantly appeared in the progress of the present work, has

creation of an enlightened anarchy. In this state each man will walk by the sole law of a reason intensely individual in its promptings, yet making inevitably for universal benevolence.

It is hardly necessary to draw attention to the fallacies of this philosophy, except in so far as Shelley's realization of them may have determined him in the subsequent reaction which succeeded his youthful devotion to Godwinism. Apart from the initial fallacy concerning the natural equality, or quasi-equality, intellectual and spiritual, of man, it is obviously ridiculous to invite him to apply his reason and will to the regeneration of a universe of which he is part, and which has already been declared subject to the law of necessity. Kant had resolved the eternal conflict between necessity and free-will by making the empirical world subject to mechanical law, from which all rational beings, as citizens of an intelligible world, were exempt and free. The individual could not control that law, though he could control his own relations to it. Godwin was incapable of the Kantian reconciliation, having indeed at his disposal no higher metaphysic whereunder to subsume and reconcile logical conceptions apparently in conflict. He therefore falls into the fallacy of making the human will operative, not only in its own Olympian sphere, but in the Titanic realm of necessity. Hating mysticism, and incapable of transcendental vision, he fell back on sentimentalism, and tried to give it a basis in 'reason'. His aspiration was a noble one: it might also have been a helpful one had he not endeavoured to

mischiefs of various sorts incorporated with its substance, and no otherwise to be removed than by its utter annihilation.' (*Political Justice*, Book V, chap 24.)

apply 'common sense' to conceptions demanding a sense by no means common.

VII

It was precisely through his possession of this latter sense that Shelley's faith and teaching ultimately became things utterly different from the Godwinian speculation. It is true that in *Queen Mab*, and indeed throughout a great deal of Shelley's poetry, we find developed the mechanical conception of perfectibility, through which a man, by taking thought, may add cubit on cubit to his spiritual stature till it is stretched to gigantic proportions. Yet even in *Queen Mab* a non-Godwinian distinction implying a difference *in kind*, not in mere condition or degree, is drawn between 'man that shall hereafter be' and 'man as vice has made him now'. The present generations are compared to leaves scattered from their tree by the autumn wind, and 'loading with loathsome rottenness the land,' which they yet fertilize

Till from the breathing lawn a forest springs
Of youth, integrity and loveliness.

To the promise of the new age many things were conceived as contributing. It was at this time Shelley's conviction that much of man's misery sprang from his having taken to unnatural habits, and, in especial, to the eating of animal food. He sings the praise of vegetarianism in one passage of the poem, and develops it prosaically and at length in one of his notes. On the other hand, natural appetite must be freed, and 'Passion's fearless wing' become unfettered. As has been already shown, this insistence on the ethical worth of passion, and its all-importance in any scheme of the

world's reform, is very characteristic of Shelley, and it
recurs henceforth throughout his poetry. Reason also
must prevail, no longer seared 'with the brand of God':
and reason will bring men health and liberty, will
abolish poverty, famine, and penal punishment, will make
the smiling earth supply all men's wants from her
bounty, and will even assuage the sting of death. Men
and women will live together perfected in love, since

> birth and life and death, and that strange state
> Before the naked soul has found its home,
> All tend to perfect happiness, and urge
> The restless wheels of being on their way,
> Whose flashing spokes, instinct with infinite life,
> Bicker and burn to gain their destined goal.

In all this there is but little which is out of keeping
with the mainly mechanical conceptions of perfectibility
which we have noticed as having occurred in certain
previous philosophies, but the belief in regeneration,
here, as in Shelley's later poetry, is by no means
confined to the sway of reason or the sphere of mankind.
The new perfection is mystical no less than mechanical.
Earth itself partakes in the change and is renewed
in bounty and glory: the icy poles are thawed and made
fruitful by the zephyrs of the south: the parched desert
becomes green and lush and habitable. The wild and
pathless ocean is begemmed with bright garden isles

> With lightsome clouds and shining seas between,
> And fertile valleys resonant with bliss.
> .   .   .   .
> All things are recreated, and the flame
> Of consentaneous love inspires all life.

And all this new beneficence, be it noted, is at this stage
of Shelley's belief achieved under the sway of necessity
and is the 'glorious prize of blindly working will.'

In *The Revolt of Islam*, as in *Hellas*, the cosmic aspect

of regeneration is, from the nature of the case, not
so prominent as it is in *Queen Mab* and *Prometheus
Unbound.* In Laone's song, in Canto V, Equality
is hailed as the eldest of things, to which even Wisdom
and Love are but slaves. It is she who has brought
about the new order :

My brethren, we are free! the plains and mountains,
The gray sea-shore, the forests and the fountains,
Are haunts of happiest dwellers;—man and woman,
  Their common bondage burst, may freely borrow
  From lawless love a solace for their sorrow;
For oft we still must weep, since we are human.
  A stormy night's serenest morrow,
  Whose showers are pity's gentle tears,
    Whose clouds are smiles of those that die
  Like infants without hopes or fears,
    And whose beams are joys that lie
  In blended hearts, now holds dominion;
The dawn of mind, which upwards on a pinion
Borne, swift as sunrise, far illumines space,
And clasps this barren world in its own bright
    embrace!

The admission that sorrow will exist, even in the golden
age, is the expression of a reaction in Shelley's soul
against his high mood of hope—a reaction which, without prevailing utterly, becomes increasingly marked in
his later poetry, and inspires his great lyrics of despair.
In the concluding stanza of the Song there is a recurrence of the belief that earth will share in the emancipation of man :

  Victory! Victory! Earth's remotest shore,
Regions which groan beneath the Antarctic stars,
  The green lands cradled in the roar
Of western waves, and wildernesses
  Peopled and vast, which skirt the oceans
Where morning dyes her golden tresses,
  Shall soon partake our high emotions:
Kings shall turn pale! Almighty Fear

The Fiend-God, when our charmèd name he hear,
  Shall fade like shadow from his thousand fanes
While Truth with Joy enthroned o'er his lost empire
    reigns!

This belief finds its most inspired expression in the
Third and Fourth Acts of *Prometheus Unbound*. Here
the great hour has come when Prometheus, the incarnation of all that is benign and inspired in man, witnesses
the liberation of the universe from Jupiter, who represents all that is tyrannous and false in the conception
of deity. Jupiter sinks into the abyss in the grasp of
Demogorgon who is at once Destiny and Eternity, and
something more mysterious still. Then comes the great
regeneration or transfiguration of the Universe, heralded
by the Earth herself, and the Spirits of the Earth and of
the Hour. It is noteworthy of the growing tendency
of Shelley's mind that the new influence first penetrates
Earth and fills her with joy and glory, and then spreads
from her to man, whereas the converse had been the
case in *The Revolt of Islam*:

                        I hear, I feel;
Thy lips are on me, and their touch runs down
Even to the adamantine central gloom
Along these marble nerves; 'tis life, 'tis joy,
And through my withered, old and icy frame
The warmth of an immortal youth shoots down
Circling. Henceforth the many children fair
Folded in my sustaining arms; all plants,
And creeping forms, and insects rainbow-winged,
And birds, and beasts, and fish, and human shapes,
Which drew disease and pain from my wan bosom,
Draining the poison of despair, shall take
And interchange sweet nutriment; to me
Shall they become like sister-antelopes
By one fair dam, snow-white and swift as wind,
Nursed among lilies near a brimming stream.

The dew-mists of my sunless sleep shall float
Under the stars like balm: night-folded flowers
Shall suck unwithering hues in their repose:
And men and beasts in happy dreams shall gather
Strength for the coming day, and all its joy:
And death shall be the last embrace of her
Who takes the life she gave, even as a mother
Folding her child, says, 'Leave me not again.'

In the following scene the Spirit of Earth describes the
transformation as it affects Nature, man, woman, beast,
and reptile; and then follows Shelley's greatest picture
of the felicity and goodness which the human race may
hope to compass:

                    but soon I looked,
And behold, thrones were kingless, and men walked
One with the other even as spirits do,
None fawned, none trampled; hate, disdain or fear,
Self-love, or self-contempt, on human brows
No more inscribed, as o'er the gate of hell,
'All hope abandon ye who enter here;'
None frowned, none trembled, none with eager fear
Gazed on another's eyes of cold command,
Until the subject of a tyrant's will
Became, worse fate, the abject of his own,
Which spurred him, like an outspent horse, to
    death.
None wrought his lips in truth-entangling lines
Which smiled the lie his tongue disdained to speak;
None, with firm sneer, trod out in his own heart
The sparks of love and hope, till there remained
Those bitter ashes, a soul self-consumed,
And the wretch crept a vampire among men,
Infecting all with his own hideous ill;
None talked that common, false, cold, hollow talk
Which makes the heart deny the *yes* it breathes,
Yet question that unmeant hypocrisy
With such a self-mistrust as has no name.
And women, too, frank, beautiful, and kind
As the free heaven which rains fresh light and dew

On the wide earth, past; gentle radiant forms,
From custom's evil taint exempt and pure;
Speaking the wisdom once they could not think,
Looking emotions once they feared to feel,
And changed to all which once they dared not be,
Yet being now, made earth like heaven; nor pride,
Nor jealousy, nor envy, nor ill shame,
The bitterest of those drops of treasured gall,
Spoilt the sweet taste of the nepenthe, love.

This latter passage doubtless owes something to
Godwin's praise of sincerity (*Political Justice*, IV. 6);
but its general setting, as supplied in the previous
passage, is mystical and totally unGodwinian. If this
mystical conception of the new order transcends the
ordinary facts of human experience and even of human
expectation, it is noteworthy that his very transcendentalism has enabled Shelley to avoid the inhuman conception of a state of perfection to be achieved after some
mysterious fashion under the dispensation of necessity,
and through the operation of mechanical reason. Two
things, moreover, must be borne in mind in relation to
the picture he here presents. In the first place man,
though transfigured and exempt from guilt and pain, is
not exempt from chance and death and mutability: and
in the second place, he has been liberated, not by the
conscious and calculating process of reason, but by the
cosmic and spontaneous operation of love. Miracle has
superseded syllogism: yet the miracle remains human
in so far as it satisfies the highest hopes and aspirations
of all humanity. We shall have more to say of it later,
in a slightly different relation.

Prometheus, through its theme and setting, is the
most symbolic and the most remote from ordinary life of
all the poems embodying Shelley's faith. Of that faith

the Fourth Act is the faithful and impassioned expression. Here more than anywhere we shall miss the truth if we try to reduce to system what was written by way of ecstasy, or make a syllogism of the choral song of the Hours and the Spirits of the Sun and Moon. On the other hand, as our examination of Shelley's other poems must certainly have shown us, the conception of love as regenerating not man alone but the universe, is not merely due to the ideal and mythological setting of the play: it recurs throughout all his poetry, and is evident even in such poems as *Hellas* where poetry actually blends with politics. And in no context in which it occurs can it be dismissed as a mere flight of poetic fancy, or disregarded in any estimate of Shelley's belief. It was an article of his faith that the universe was informed by a single all-pervading spirit and that any change in any part of that spirit must affect the whole. In the Third Act, as we have seen, the Universe had become interpenetrated with beneficence and love, and this benign influence had spread from it to man. In the Fourth Act, we have at once the converse and the sequel: the Universe, after its transfiguration, becomes subject to the Spirit of humanity—humanity now regarded as one instead of many:

> Man, oh, not men! a chain of linkèd thought,
>   Of love and might to be divided not,
> Compelling the elements with adamantine stress;
>   As the sun rules, even with a tyrant's gaze,
>   The unquiet republic of the maze
> Of planets, struggling fierce towards heaven's free
>   wilderness.
>
> Man, one harmonious soul of many a soul,
>   Whose nature is its own divine control
> Where all things flow to all, as rivers to the sea;

Familiar acts are beautiful through love;
Labour, and pain, and grief, in life's green grove
Sport like tame beasts, none knew how gentle they
could be![1]

This is the consummation toward which all humankind
is unconsciously striving; and both the striving and the
consummation find fervent expression at the close of the
Prometheus, and again in *Adonais*, *Mont Blanc*, and
Hellas. To elaborate this article of Shelley's faith, or
attempt to explain it in detail, would be to darken its
true light and meaning, and would be almost as unhelpful
as to regard it as a mere poetic ecstasy of the moment.
Its significance in relation to the more obvious aspects
of his belief may be seen from its recurrence in the
culminating passage of *Prometheus*:

To suffer woes which Hope thinks infinite;
To forgive wrongs darker than death or night;
  To defy Power, which seems omnipotent;
To love, and bear; to hope till Hope creates
From its own wreck the thing it contemplates;
  Neither to change, nor falter, nor repent;
This, like thy glory, Titan, is to be
Good, great and joyous, beautiful and free;
This is alone Life, Joy, Empire and Victory.

---

[1] Cf. Swinburne, *Hymn of Man*:

Past the wall unsurmounted that bars out our vision with iron
    and fire
He hath sent forth his soul for the stars to comply with and
    suns to conspire,
His thought takes flight for the centre wherethrough it hath
    part in the whole;
The abysses forbid it not enter: the stars make room for the
    soul.
Space is the soul's to inherit; the night is hers as the day;
Lo, saith man, this is my spirit: how shall not the worlds
    make way?
Space is thought's and the wonders thereof, and the secret of
    space;
Is thought not more than the thunders and lightnings? Shall
    thought give place?

VIII

In *Hellas* occurs again the conception of a Golden Ag,
of the future, together with a further conception, fairly
marked in much of Shelley's other poetry, that that Age
had been heralded by a Golden Age in the past.
Shelley's admiration for ancient Greece, and his hope
for the regeneration of modern Greece, made it natural
for him to connect the two Ages through this particular
country and race. 'We are all Greeks,' he says in the
Preface to this poem : 'our laws, our literature, our
religion, our arts, have their roots in Greece.' In the
mighty chorus beginning 'In the great morning of the
world', freedom is traced from its first liberation by the
Spirit of God at Marathon and Thermopylae, through
its recurrent visitations to earth in 'Florence, Albion,
Switzerland, utmost Germany and Spain', till the time of
that triumphant appearance which should free its ancient
stronghold from Turkish domination. In the final
chorus the modern freedom of Greece is augured from
the vision of her ancient freedom, though the sequel is
infinitely more beautiful and glorious than its archetype :

> The world's great age begins anew,
>   The golden years return,
> The earth doth like a snake renew
>   Her winter weeds outworn:
> Heaven smiles, and faiths and empires gleam,
> Like wrecks of a dissolving dream.
>
> A brighter Hellas rears its mountains
>   From waves serener far ;
> A new Peneus rolls his.fountains
>   Against the morning star.
> Where fairer Tempes bloom, there sleep
> Young Cyclads on a sunnier deep.
>   .   .   .   .

Another Athens shall arise,
  And to remoter time
Bequeath, like sunset to the skies,
  The splendour of its prime;
And leave, if nought so bright may live,
All earth can take or Heaven can give.

Saturn and Love their long repose
  Shall burst, more bright and good
Than all who fell, than One who rose,
  Than many unsubdued:
Not gold, not blood, their altar dowers,
But votive tears and symbol flowers.

In his conception of a Golden Age of the past, Shelley
was doubtless influenced, not only by his admiration for
Greece, but by the conception, which finds its most
notable expression in Rousseau, of an early condition of
the world in which innocence and simplicity prevailed,
to be marred and foiled by the selfish gregariousness
and sophistication of 'civilized' man. With Shelley,
however, freedom, though latent in the scheme of things,
is not regarded as being actually realized in a primaeval
condition of the world. On the contrary, as is shown in
the *Ode to Liberty*, the spirit of Nature in the beginning
was 'a chaos and a curse' for the lack of liberty:

                  power from worst producing worse,
The spirit of the beasts was kindled there,
  And of the birds, and of the watery forms,
And there was war among them, and despair
  Within them, raging without truce or terms.

Similarly man:

This human living multitude
Was savage, cunning, blind, and rude.

The devotees of thought and beauty yearned for the new
spirit; but it did not come till the rise of Athens, which
renewed the world with delight, and was the earthly
pattern of that 'one spirit vast' which 'with life and love

makes chaos ever new'. The vicissitudes of the world
and her fitful redemptions by liberty are traced onwards
through Rome, England, Italy, and Germany, till she is
summoned to awake and cast off the odious dominion of
priest and king,

> Till human thoughts might kneel alone,
> Each before the judgement-throne
> Of its own aweless soul, or of the Power unknown!

Throughout this poem we find recurring Shelley's keen
sense of the kinship of liberty with beauty, the beauty
in the case of Greece being that of plastic art. In the
following stanza Liberty is actually the creator of the
fair statues and temples of Athens:

> Athens arose: a city such as vision
>   Builds from the purple crags and silver towers
> Of battlemented cloud, as in derision
>   Of kingliest masonry: the ocean-floors
> Pave it; the evening sky pavilions it;
>   Its portals are inhabited
>   By thunder-zonèd winds, each head
> Within its cloudy wings with sun-fire garlanded,—
>   A divine work! Athens, diviner yet,
>   Gleamed with its crest of columns, on the will
> Of man, as on a mount of diamond, set;
>   For thou wert, and thine all-creative skill
> Peopled, with forms that mock the eternal dead
>   In marble immortality, that hill
> Which was thine earliest throne and latest oracle.

In a later stanza we are told that 'Art which cannot die'
co-operated in Italy's struggle for freedom, and

> With divine wand traced on our earthly home
> Fit imagery to pave Heaven's everlasting dome.

And later still Art is hailed as

>   an ardent intercessor,
> Driving on fiery wings to Nature's throne.

IX

The world's regeneration, however, according to Shelley, depends on something more than a Golden Age in the past which the future will recapture and outgo. He constantly expresses his belief that the principle of beneficence *already exists* in the nature of things, and is only waiting to be brought to light, and freed from the fettering and obscuring mechanism of ordinary life. Its fitful visitations are due to a partial lifting of the veil which at present conceals it from humanity. Were this veil wholly lifted, all beauty, charity, and truth would be at once realized. It is of the first moment, for the understanding of his faith, to realize the intensity of this conviction and its constant recurrence throughout his poetry. The new order of things, in his view, was not to be realized through the action of a mechanical logic offering social syllogisms to a suffering and yearning world. There could be no arithmetical progression toward right, since there was an initial flaw in the sum of things as displayed on the blackboard of the present order. There could be no hope in a gradual building up upon a foundation demonstrably rotten. The new order must be won, not through calculation but through conversion, through a passionate intuition of the worth and beauty inherent in the nature of things, and only obscured from man by the veil of his present life. The word and the idea of the Veil occur constantly through-out Shelley's poetry, with a significance which is explained elsewhere in this volume; but it is important for our present purpose to notice that, though it some-times signifies merely the obscurantism of worldly convention, it generally implies far more than this, and means a cosmic fabric alien to the truer and higher nature of the universe—a fabric which must be rent asunder so that the inner truth and beauty of things may be made manifest. This conception appears already in *The Daemon of the World*:

> Majestic spirit, be it thine
> The flame to seize, the veil to rend,
> Where the vast snake Eternity
> In charmèd sleep doth ever lie.
> . . . .
> Spirit, leave for mine and me
> Earth's unsubstantial mimicry!

And toward the end it recurs in the famous lines of *Prometheus*:

> The painted veil, by those who were, called life,
> Which mimicked, as with colours idly spread,
> All men believed or hoped, is torn aside;
> The loathsome mask has fallen.

Constantly, as in the passage just quoted from *The Daemon of the World*, Eternity, the reality, is contrasted with Time, the thwarting and often malignant shadow. It is so again in *The Daemon of the World*:

> Thou hoary giant Time,
> Render thou up thy half-devourèd babes,—
> And from the cradles of eternity,
> Where millions lie lulled to their portioned sleep
> By the deep murmuring stream of passing things,
> Tear thou that gloomy shroud.

The indictment of Time appears under a more personal and poignant form in the lyric with *Time* for its title:

> Unfathomable Sea! whose waves are years,
> Ocean of Time, whose waters of deep woe
> Are brackish with the salt of human tears!

Similarly, in *Hellas*, Mahmud refers to 'this gloomy crag of time to which I cling'. In the same drama the

Future and the Past are dismissed by Ahasuerus as
' idle shadows of thought's eternal flight' : neither they,
nor

> this Whole
> Of suns, and worlds, and men, and beasts, and
>   flowers,
> With all the silent or tempestuous workings
> By which they have been, are, or cease to be,

have power to affect the Universal Spirit—' the One, the
unborn and the undying'. In this passage certain human
attributes are exempted from the transitoriness of things
born in Time:

> Thought
> Alone, and its quick elements, Will, Passion,
> Reason, Imagination, cannot die ;
> They are, what that which they regard appears,
> The stuff whence mutability can weave
> All that it hath dominion o'er, worlds, worms,
> Empires and superstitions.

Similarly in *Prometheus* Time is described as the
' envious shadow' which fell from the throne of Saturn ;
and at the world's regeneration Time, the King of the
Hours, is borne to his tomb in Eternity. Again, in the
final chorus of the drama, Gentleness, Virtue, Wisdom,
and Endurance are portrayed as the potential saviours of
Eternity, ' mother of many acts and hours', from ' the
serpent that would clasp her with its length'. In certain
famous lines of *Adonais*, the antithesis between time and
eternity is again evident, and here, too, Shelley
emphasizes his belief that the spirit of love, the regenerating force of the universe, is single and universal, and
has its true existence independent of the thwarting
shows of the phenomenal world :

> The One remains, the many change and pass ;
> Heaven's light forever shines, Earth's shadows fly ;

> Life, like a dome of many-coloured glass,
> Stains the white radiance of Eternity,
> Until Death tramples it to fragments.

Shelley almost universally refers to Time as a force in some sense thwarting good and favouring evil, to which it is seemingly akin.   As he regards evil as a thing which must disappear from the earth, we must probably not regard him as attacking Time in its literal significance, but only in so far as he regards it as a symbol of the present order.   His insistence that Time must be transcended before the new and fairer order can be achieved, shows how fundamental, in his opinion, must be the nature of the change.   But his association of evil with Time shows that he did not, as some have said, regard evil as a mere accretion of human chance or ignorance or prejudice, as something which would disappear mechanically when argument or force was brought to bear on it.   It was not an accident of life, but a principle: it was inherent in things—inherent at any rate in their present order.   If we must not seek for a fully developed system in the inspired utterances of poetry, this much at least was an essential of Shelley's belief, and, as we shall see, it is closely bound up with his sense of the sinister in life.   We have already emphasized his belief in the dual principles of oppression and goodness as he saw them incarnate in the eagle and the snake.   Behind 'the painted veil which those who live call life' there lurked Fear as well as Hope [1]: and with Shelley, Fear passed in many moods into Despair—

> The guardian angel gone,
> The daemon reassumed his throne
> In my faint heart.

[1] Sonnet published by Mrs. Shelley, *Posthumous Poems*, 1824.

This despair was elemental with him: it inspired some of his most intense poetry; and it is not to be explained as a mere conviction that man's endeavour is at present thwarted by the play of superficial and easily remediable accident. Not in this mood was written the apostrophe to Time:

> Thou shoreless flood, which in thy ebb and flow
> Claspest the limits of mortality,
> And sick of prey, yet howling on for more,
> Vomitest thy wrecks on its inhospitable shore;
> Treacherous in calm, and terrible in storm,
> Who shall put forth on thee,
> Unfathomable Sea?

The *Stanzas written in Dejection near Naples*, and the *Invocation to Misery* might, perhaps, be dismissed as mere subjective expressions of a passing mood: but there are far too many 'fervours and recurrences' in Shelley's poetry of despondency to admit of our attributing the whole of this to mere fleeting impressionism. Such an interpretation will not explain the poem just quoted, nor yet the *Dirge*, with its burden of cosmic woe:

> Rough wind, that moanest loud
> Grief too sad for song;
> Wild wind, when sullen cloud
> Knells all the night long;
> Sad storm, whose tears are vain,
> Bare woods, whose branches strain,
> Deep caves and dreary main,—
> Wail, for the world's wrong!

X

It may, perhaps, seem difficult to reconcile this conception of evil with Shelley's belief in human perfectibility: and it might perhaps be claimed that such reconciliation is unnecessary in poetry, the high region of unresolved antinomies. It is, however, certain that

Shelley believed that evil, if it is positive and deep-rooted, is also eradicable. It can be made to disappear from life, and, given the necessary condition of the change, there need be little transformation of the present order :

                                    and soon
Those ugly human shapes and visages
Of which I spoke as having wrought me pain,
Passed floating through the air, and fading still
Into the winds that scattered them ; and those
From whom they passed seemed mild and lovely forms
After some foul disguise had fallen, and all
Were somewhat changed, and after brief surprise
And greetings of delighted wonder, all
Went to their sleep again : and when the dawn
Came, wouldst thou think that toads, and snakes,
    and efts,
Could e'er be beautiful ? yet so they were,
And that with little change of shape or hue :
All things had put their evil nature off.

Despite Shelley's sense of the deeprootedness of evil, we are haunted throughout his writings by the feeling that it is only the thinnest of divisions which separates the ideal world of joy and truth and beauty from the actual one in which cruelty and hypocrisy have sway : and in this relation, too, his favourite symbol of the Veil has profound significance.   The new order is to be achieved by some process far more elemental and compulsive than syllogistic reasoning.   Perhaps the best word to explain this process, as it is described in the sequence of Shelley's longer poems, would be conversion—conversion having in it a more profound and ecstatic quality than the mere Platonic turning of the eyes to the light—conversion operating not, as in certain religions, for the negation of passion, but through its aid and for its sub-limer affirmation.   This conversion was to be achieved,

not through the preaching of olden morality nor yet
through the mere acquisition of modern knowledge,
but through the birth in universal humanity of a new
sense. This sense would bring with it utter charity and
truth and understanding; and it would do this by making
each one feel himself a participant in a unity comprising
all humankind and all creation, a unity which must be
injured in all its parts by injury or injustice done to any
one of its members, till, if we may so put the matter, a
man might be withheld from transgression against his
neighbour by the thought,

> Is it not as this mouth should tear this hand
> For lifting food to't?

Shelley's many descriptions of the means by which
the new order is to be achieved are obviously ideal, and
to some they may seem to be nothing but a beautiful
allegory, a sublime reminder of the higher spiritual
being latent in all humanity. Those who take this
view will consider his teaching as rather a monition than
a prophecy, and only as such will they assent to it. It
is certain, however, that Shelley himself regarded it in
no such light, but firmly believed that the regeneration
of man could, and would, eventually be accomplished.
Since his day the mighty issues interwoven with his
song have been given fresh meaning by a factor which
he could not have divined or suspected. The doctrine
of evolution, whether it be interpreted materially or
ideally, has shown the history of life to be a progress
from lower to higher through ordered and distinct stages.
At certain of these stages the progress has not been
merely one of growth and modification, but has resulted
in the appearance of a new faculty, and consequently
of an order differing utterly and in kind from the old.

By such a process did organic life evolve from inorganic, consciousness from the unconscious, freewill from the determinate. The evolution of each of these faculties implied the evolution of a new stage and order in the existing scheme of things. And if any conjecture as to the future may be warranted by the whole history of the past, if there be any worth in any human process of analogy, evolution will continue, and will result in generic change. There is obviously, however, a vast distinction between the primal stages of evolution and that existing stage which has found its highest expression in man. In the earlier forms, life was determined by the operation of forces which it could not consciously control : but man's evolution now lies largely in his own hands, and his future cannot be moulded save by aid of his own consciousness and freewill. Even if he wished to do so, he could not leave his future development to the mercy of blind chance, or of any cosmic principle of which he was the mere plaything. He must at least have a hand in the spinning of his future fate. What determination his destiny may take has been a matter of doubt and contradiction. Some hold that progress lies through the combating of Nature, others believe that it can only be realized through obedience to her bidding. To some it has seemed that man can only rise above himself by becoming superman, by ensuing ruthlessness and strength, and crushing out the more soft and tender qualities of his nature. To these, the Christian ethic seems contemptible, not, as in Shelley's view, for its abuses, but in its very nature and essence. Nietzsche and Shelley both attacked Christianity fiercely : but the causes of their antipathy are not so much different as diametrically opposed. Nietzsche

attacked Christ's personality and the spirit of his teaching, and exalted the Old Testament as the gospel of
ruthlessness and force: Shelley, on the other hand,
hated and attacked the Old Testament dispensation, and
exempted the personality and spirit of Christ alone from
his attacks on Christianity. Most of the highest modern
thought is opposed to Nietzsche's theory of the future
of the race, and conceives the possibility of progress
as lying, not in increased ruthlessness, but in the evolution of a keener sense of charity and love and understanding. To those who hold this belief, Christianity
appears to be not only a symbol of what is most beneficent in the past, but the symbol, too, of the future
beneficence which life must necessarily realize if man,
its supreme expression, only develops according to the
highest law and prompting that are within him. To
those who have divined the teaching of the past, such
an evolution will seem the process not of years nor of
centuries, but of aeons. As has happened heretofore,
it must be built upon striving and failure and renewed
striving, must be achieved in the teeth of such manifold
frustrations as we see to-day in our world of common
life. But to those who have learnt the 'lesson of the
flesh' and are undeterred as they mark by 'what slow
degrees the world-soul quickens through the centuries',
there seems good hope of such fruition. And if it be
true, as Shelley thought, that love is the highest and
strongest thing in the human soul, if it be through love
that soul is to reach its highest development, may we
not justly conjecture the mode of that development
from the pattern of the past? The evolution of life has
in certain of its past stages resulted in the birth of new
faculties differing utterly and in kind from the old: does

not the hope of the future lie in the belief that there, too, there will be a similar birth ? And if the progress of the race be ethical, if it make for the fuller development of man's moral power and worth, for an immensely heightened faculty of his love and sympathy, is there not likelihood of a generic change in his nature, to be effected through these causes and for this end ? Does not a survey of the past and the present indicate that the future may well bring forth a special sense in which each man will literally feel his neighbour's suffering and joy as his own, and be incapable of hurting him without himself feeling the smart ?

> Leaf shall of leaf become aware
> On the selfsame bough and stem,
> Whose branches are murmuring everywhere,
> And the heaven floods all of them!
> Between you—*between all that live*—
> Runs no gulf wide nor deep—
> But a sheened veil, thinner than any veil,
> Thin as the veil of sleep.[1]

The possibility of such a development is no fanciful one, for it has all the lesson of the past to warrant it. Despite certain black periods of the world's history, despite man's frequent lapses from grace, all but the complete cynic and pessimist would recognize an ever-increasing humanitarianism in his history since his evolution from his earliest stages: and this growth might well afford a guarantee that such a new sense as we have discussed is already in the making. In its creation a leading part has, of course, been taken, and certainly will be taken, by Reason ; but not by the Godwinian Reason, which ignores the mystical element in man, and pretends that it can effect its purpose by mere demonstration, on the assumption that man is an auto-

[1] Herbert Trench, *Apollo and the Seaman.*

maton and evil an accidental accretion of life. Were this new sense once fully developed, Shelley's hope and faith would at once be realized, and the world's great age would have begun anew. Considered in this sense, *Prometheus* and *Hellas* contain much more than an exquisite reminder given to man of an ideal which he will never realize, but which it is good for him occasion-ally to behold. They contain the actual symbol of that which may yet be—which, indeed, must be—if man's progress, despite its imperfections and frustrations, be on the whole an upward one making for an increased love of his kind. Time, the only means of achieving the new order, is also 'the universal wonder-hider' and interposes its aeons between conception and fruition: and it is surely for this cause that Shelley rails at it so fiercely. If its slow malignancy be regarded as the determining factor in existence, there may seem to be little encouragement or worth in his intense conviction that the ideal beneficence is only separated from the ugliness and pettiness of the actual by the thinness of a Veil. But if life be regarded in a more absolute relationship, if it be conceived according to the law of its whole past history as in transition from lower to higher, a different view is possible. The seed of the higher and happier future will be felt to be already latent in the order of the present: and though generic change will have to occur before its fruition, there will be justi-fication for that curious sense of *nearness* between the old order and the new which is so constant in Shelley's poetry. The present already holds the future

> like unfolded flowers beneath the sea,
> Like the man's thought dark in the infant's brain,
> Like aught that is which wraps what is to be.

Time for a while shall thwart the realization of the new happiness and glory: but in the end the Hours shall bear him to his tomb in Eternity, and

> Saturn and Love their long repose
>   Shall burst, more bright and good
> Than all who fell, than One who rose,
>   Than many unsubdued:
> Not gold, not blood, their altar dowers,
> But votive tears and symbol flowers.

SHELLEY'S SYMBOLISM

I

The word 'symbolism' might be used, with reference to Shelley, in several distinct senses. It might indicate his normal and deliberate use of abstraction or image, and might in this sense include the personified forces of life and nature which we meet in *Adonais*, or the gods and demigods, the spirits and the furies of *Prometheus Unbound*, or the powers of *Hellas* who from their 'thrones pinnacled on the past sway the reluctant present'. If we used the word in this sense it would be necessary to re-survey Shelley's poetry of Nature, to recapture its imagery, and to discover, if we could, in what sense this was the expression of his general intuition of the universe. The exultation of Earth at her liberation in *Prometheus*, the dance of joy woven by the Hours on the floor of the breeze, the grief of Spring for lost Adonais, her throwing down 'her kindling buds as if she Autumn were', the charioting of the winged seeds to their dark wintry bed by the West Wind, and their reawakening when Autumn's 'azure sister' blows 'her clarion o'er the dreaming earth'—all of these things are exquisite symbols of Shelley's faith. To see their full significance, it would be necessary to discuss that faith in detail, and to relate it to these several shapes or images. But the significance of this kind of imagery in Shelley is for the most part obvious, and in so far as it is not so, it has been discussed in the first essay of this volume in relation to his general beliefs. Though reference will be made throughout the present essay both to these beliefs and to such imagery as we have just discussed, it is a special variety of Shelley's symbolism with which we are here immediately concerned.

Nothing is more characteristic of his poetry than the recurrence throughout it of certain definite ideas and images, and even of certain significant words and phrases. In the case of some writers, such recurrence might be ascribed to poverty of imagination, to the literary parsimony which deliberately repeats a tried and effective phrase or conception. Such an explanation, however, is ludicrously inadequate to the case of Shelley, who was as intellectually scrupulous, and as little addicted to deliberate self-plagiarism, as he was fertile in new and exquisite imaginings. In prose, and especially in prose where the highest imaginative power is in abeyance, such repetition is generally conscious, and is frequently, indeed, self-conscious. In this case it may tell us comparatively little regarding its author's inmost nature. But in poetry, consciousness is the mere instrument of the unconscious mind, which in the ferment of poetic creation throws up the inmost secrets of its author's being. These secrets are sometimes so unfamiliar to the poet's conscious self as to strike him as the creation of another personality : yet if he finds that what comes to him from the subconscious is alien to his own convictions, he has always the chance and right of rejecting it : for all true poetry is a review and selection made by consciousness of images flung up by the unconscious from its hidden caverns. Attempts have recently been made, through methods claiming to be scientific, to seize on this evidence presented by the conscious mind, and through it to make the unconscious reveal its secrets; and in certain cases this method has been applied to imaginative literature. Such a process of investigation, depending as it does on the application to poetry of knowledge, or theory, assumed to be medical, may easily result in fantastic conclusions: and the present essayist has no ambition to submit the spirit of Shelley to a scientific, or pseudo-scientific, cross-examination in 'third degree'. It may fairly be claimed, however, that if the same image recurs constantly in such poetry as Shelley's, where the poet is writing with passionate intensity, and pouring out at white heat the stream of his inmost thought, that image represents something more than a mere verbal echo or reiterated intellectual conceit, and corresponds to a profound spiritual conviction—a conviction reaching deeper than the level of consciousness. And when such an image has definite relation to other imagery in the poet's writings, and has direct bearing on the main articles of his conscious faith, right understanding of its meaning becomes a matter of some importance.

As has been shown elsewhere in this volume, it was a deep-rooted conviction of Shelley's that the visible world was only a half-real approximation to the full reality of the invisible world—from which it was nevertheless separated only by the thinnest of partitions. Once the partition were rent asunder, and men saw life, and one another, face to face, there was every promise that they would cease from suspicion and war and hatred and would love and trust each other, thus renewing the 'world's great age'. Such a conviction as this, looking as it does to a kind of world-convulsion and conversion, is, as we have contended elsewhere, an utterly different thing from the belief of William Godwin that a new order could be achieved through a progressive series of syllogisms. Fresh light may perhaps be thrown on Shelley's view of the world's regeneration if we discuss briefly the use which he constantly makes of the symbol of the Veil.

II

Shelley uses this word and image fairly freely, even in the immature verse of his youth, and though the ideas which it here expresses are less definite and specialized than those which he ultimately attached to it, their significance is the same. Thus in *A Dialogue*, Death, in refusing the Mortal's appeal for liberation, replies:

> Cease, cease, wayward Mortal! I dare not unveil
> The shadows that float o'er Eternity's vale.

In the *Retrospect*, the 'mild glances' of affection's eye

> Pierce the thin veil of flesh that shrouds
> The spirit's inmost sanctuary.

In *Queen Mab*, the Fairy declares

> And it is yet permitted me, to rend
> The veil of mortal frailty, that the spirit,
> Clothed in its changeless purity, may know
> How soonest to accomplish the great end
> For which it hath its being, and may taste
> That peace, which in the end all life will share.

In certain other passages Shelley speaks of 'Eternity's veil', meaning not the veil which is Eternity, but the veil—constantly identified in his later poetry with Time—which obscures Eternity from the sight of man. This point is made plain in that rehandling of the earlier part of

Queen Mab known as *The Daemon of the World*.   Here
Shelley writes:

> There from nature's inner shrine,
>   Where gods and fiends in worship bend,
> Majestic spirit, be it thine
>   The flame to seize, the veil to rend,
>   Where the vast snake Eternity
>   In charmèd sleep doth ever lie.

In the last two of the three passages first quoted,
Shelley, in considering the body as that which obscures
the light and truth of the spirit, is partly following his
beloved Plato, partly obeying the other-worldly instinct
of his own nature.   In another passage of *Queen Mab*,
the Veil is the flimsy pretence of justice and right
behind which selfishness conceals 'its unattractive
lineaments, that scare all save the brood of ignorance'.
It is equally malign with the Veil of the previous
instances, though here it obscures evil rather than good.
Later in the same poem the Veil is once more considered
as the sinister disguise of evil—the disguise of humanity
in which the malignant deity conceals 'His horrible
Godhead'.   The remaining passage of the poem in
which the symbol is used is the complement of other
passages referring to the Veil of Eternity.   Here the
Veil of Time—i.e. the Veil which *is* Time—was rent
asunder and

> Hope was seen beaming through the mists of fear :
>   Earth was no longer Hell ;
>   Love, freedom, health, had given
> Their ripeness to the manhood of its prime,
>   And all its pulses beat
> Symphonious to the planetary spheres.

Here we have already in the germ the idea which is to
find its full fruition in *Prometheus Unbound* ; but it is

noteworthy that Shelley's use of the symbol already implies, not only contempt and distrust of the outer show of things, not only a conviction that it differs utterly and in kind from the ideal reality, but a further conviction that, despite this inexpressible difference, the division separating the two worlds is of the thinnest. Later in the poem fresh light is thrown on the inter-relation of the two worlds, and it is shown that life is only a mode—or, as Schopenhauer would have called it, the objectification—of the universal spirit:

> For birth but wakes the spirit to the sense
> Of outward shows, whose unexperienced shape
> New modes of passion to its frame may lend;
> Life is its state of action, and the store
> Of all events is aggregated there
> That variegate the eternal universe;
> Death is a gate of dreariness and gloom,
> That leads to azure isles and beaming skies
> And happy regions of eternal hope.

When we pass from Shelley's earlier verse to his maturer poetry we find the image of the Veil repeated in various contexts and with various meanings. In almost every case it is used disparagingly to express that which conceals and inhibits goodness or happiness rather than that which shelters and protects them. Occasionally, indeed, it has this latter significance, as when in *Epipsychidion* the poet looks joyously toward the consummation when he shall 'at the noontide hour arrive' with Emily

> Where some old cavern hoar seems yet to keep
> The moonlight of the expired night asleep,
> Through which the awakened day can never peep;
> A veil for our seclusion, close as night's.

It has kindred but more figurative meaning in the passage of *The Revolt of Islam* in which Cythna

> walks through the great City, veiled
> In virtue's adamantine eloquence.

But far more commonly it is used to express that which conceals truth or beauty from man. In certain cases the application is obvious. Thus Cythna says:

> With strong speech I tore the veil that hid
> Nature, and Truth, and Liberty, and Love.

The image has the same obvious meaning when the Chorus sings at the opening of *Hellas*:

> Life may change, but it may fly not;
> Hope may vanish, but can die not;
> Truth be veiled, but still it burneth;
> Love repulsed,—but it returneth!

and when, in *Epipsychidion*, the poet writes in reference to his meeting with Emilia:

> I knew it was the Vision veiled from me
> So many years—that it was Emily.

Similarly, in the same poem, Emilia is hailed as the 'veiled glory of this lampless universe'. Though none of these uses would seem peculiar if we met them in any other poet, Shelley's imagery here is probably used with a certain special significance which will become clearer if we examine a few further instances.

His fondness for the word and the idea leads him elsewhere to use them in senses that are as strange as they are effective: thus in *The Triumph of Life* 'corruption veils' the corpses 'as they lie': while a different strangeness is evident in the description given in *Alastor* of the poet's vision of his beloved:

> At the sound he turned,
> And saw by the warm light of their own life
> Her glowing limbs beneath the sinuous veil
> Of woven wind.

A common and significant variety of the symbol occurs in these lines from the *Ode to Naples*:

> From Freedom's form divine,
> From Nature's inmost shrine,
> Strip every impious gawd, rend Error veil by veil;

and in the reference in *Prometheus Unbound* to

> Swift shapes and sounds, which grow
> More fair and soft as man grows wise and kind,
> And, veil by veil, evil and error fall.

In this last passage the symbol of the Veil is used to express Shelley's conviction that goodness and beauty are the primary realities in man's nature, error and evil the less essential fabrics which conceal him from his fellows and himself. But the most important meaning of the Veil in Shelley, and the one which serves best to explain the rest, is that in which it is regarded as a symbol of life. Sometimes we have a case analogous to the one just cited: and life itself, or the present fabric of life, is conceived as a thing veiling or thwarting humanity from the achievement of its highest form of self-realization. Thus the Spirit of the Hour in *Prometheus Unbound* speaks of the world's regeneration: ·

> The painted veil, by those who were, called life,
> Which mimicked, as with colours idly spread,
> All men believed or hoped, is torn aside;
> The loathsome mask has fallen.

The fact that Shelley regards life itself, or what is ordinarily understood as life, as an obstacle to man's regeneration, shows how fundamental was the change which he regarded as necessary for the realization of the new order: and it shows also how utterly, toward the end of his life, his faith transcended the trim ratiocina-

tion of William Godwin. On the other hand, the very
fact that he portrays life in the image of the Veil shows
that he regards the fabric severing good from evil, error
from truth, as of the thinnest, and as destructible in the
very moment in which the heart of man should be
converted to desire for the change.

Generally, however, when the symbol of the Veil is
used in relation to life, a somewhat different image is
intended, and life is regarded as that which conceals the
reality, not of man's nature, but of the Universe or
Eternity. In this sense the Veil is used to express the
whole fabric or pageantry of our present existence. It
is so in the opening lines of the sonnet:

> Lift not the painted veil which those who live
> Call Life: though unreal shapes be pictured there,
> And it but mimic all we would believe
> With colours idly spread,—behind, lurk Fear
> And Hope, twin Destinies.

Here the thwarting shows of existence are contrasted
with the ideal beauty of human imagining; but it is
implied that even when human thought passes beyond
the Veil, Fear as well as Hope

> who ever weave
> Their shadows, o'er the chasm, sightless and drear,

are interposed between the seeker and the reality of his
desire. The opening line of this passage serves to
explain the more difficult passage in *Prometheus*:

> Death is the veil which those who live call life:
> They sleep and it is lifted,

where life itself is identified with death in contrast with
the reality beyond both. These two passages are very
significant of the Platonic quality of Shelley's thought

concerning life and reality. A further important passage
is that in which the poet, with the sublime and various
beauty of Mont Blanc before him, makes this conjecture
as to its meaning:

> Some say that gleams of a remoter world
> Visit the soul in sleep,—that death is slumber,
> And that its shapes the busy thoughts ·outnumber
> Of those who wake and live.—I look on high ;
> Has some unknown omnipotence unfurled
> The veil of life and death ? or do I lie
> In dream, and does the mightier world of sleep
> Spread far around and inaccessibly
> Its circles ?

Such is the text as Shelley left it: but James Thomson
('B. V.') thought it necessary to read 'upfurled' for
'unfurled', and thus to imply that in the line quoted
Shelley was conceiving himself as gazing beyond reality
into the wonder of the world beyond. The context,
however, clearly shows that Shelley intends to suggest
an alternative between the present life seen in its most
perfect manifestation, and the wonder of the world of
dream : and if regard be paid to his other uses of the
Veil to express the phenomenal world, little difficulty
will be found in the passage. He clearly here means to
ask whether he is to regard the whole beauty of this life
as being suddenly unrolled before him, or whether what
he sees is the mightier and more transcendent beauty of
the dream-world.

It is a frequent thought of Shelley's that dream,
through its kinship with Death the Revealer, offers
man a fuller vision of reality than life can supply. In
this sense, day, and light itself, are frequently regarded
as the obscuring Veil. Thus in *The Sensitive Plant*
Shelley writes:

And when evening descended from Heaven above,
And the Earth was all rest, and the air was all love,
And delight, though less bright, was far more deep,
And the day's veil fell from the world of sleep.

In one of the *Fragments of an Unfinished Drama*
sleep is regarded as the lifting of a Veil—the Veil
of ordinary waking life—from the reality of Heaven:

O friend, sleep was a veil uplift from Heaven—
As if Heaven dawned upon the world of dream.

The keenness with which Shelley felt the illusoriness of
the phenomenal world may be illustrated by the curious
distrust which he frequently shows of its informing
principle, Light. Sometimes the symbol of the Veil,
when applied to Light, is used in a neutral sense, or in
one making for beauty. Thus Shelley writes in *The
Triumph of Life*:

A strange trance over my fancy grew
Which was not slumber, for the shade it spread

Was so transparent that the scene came through
As clear as when a veil of light is drawn
O'er evening hills they glimmer.

In other cases the feeling of illusion is stronger and
suggests the idea that there is obscurity in the very
intensity of that which lends the phenomenal world its
semblance of illumination and reality. Thus in *Hellas*
the Chorus sings:

Guide us far, far, away,
To climes where now veiled by the ardour of day
Thou art hidden
From waves on which weary Noon
Faints in her summer swoon.

In *The Sensitive Plant,* the Lady, in her beauty, looks

> As if some bright Spirit for her sweet sake
> Had deserted Heaven while the stars were awake,
> As if yet around her he lingering were,
> Though the veil of daylight concealed him from her.

The same idea underlies the beauty of the image in
Hellas where the ruins of Freedom

> glow
> Like Orient mountains lost in day,

and reappears in the simile of *The Triumph of Life*:

> Some like eaglets on the wing
> Were lost in the white day.

Shelley's distrust of the light of this world appears in a
more near and obvious form in the lines of the *Letter to
Maria Gisborne* in which he tells how he and his
English friends at Leghorn

> spun
> A shroud of talk to hide us from the sun
> Of this familiar life, which seems to be
> But is not.

The conception of the *spiritual* light of our present
existence as obscuring despite, or because of, its very
intensity, is evident in the famous comparison of the
Skylark's song to

> a Poet hidden
> In the light of thought,
> Singing hymns unbidden,
> Till the world is wrought
> To sympathy with hopes and fears it heeded not.

Here there is no suggestion of distrust or disparage-
ment: but there is such a suggestion in the fragmentary
Prologue to *Hellas,* where human thought is regarded
as concealing the eternal verities:

> Hierarchs and kings
> Who from your thrones pinnacled on the past
> Sway the reluctant present, ye who sit
> Pavilioned on the radiance or the gloom
> Of mortal thought, which like an exhalation
> Steaming from earth, conceals the   [1] of heaven
> Which gave it birth.

In two cases Shelley applies the symbol of the Veil to
art, and in each case to the art of sculpture. In a
magnificent stanza of the *Ode to Liberty* he describes
Greece before the rise of Athens as big with the promise
of future glory :

> On the unapprehensive wild
>   The vine, the corn, the olive mild,
> Grew savage yet, to human use unreconciled ;
>   And, like unfolded flowers beneath the sea,
>   Like the man's thought dark in the infant's brain,
>   Like aught that is which wraps what is to be,
>   Art's deathless dreams lay veiled by many a vein
> Of Parian stone ; and, yet a speechless child,
>   Verse murmured, and Philosophy did strain
>   Her lidless eyes for thee ; when o'er the Aegean main
> Athens arose.

Here the idea of art is conceived as being already latent
in the raw material from which it will some day be
evoked. A different use is evident in one of the fragments connected with *Epipsychidion*, where Shelley
compares Emily to that 'sweet marble monster of both
sexes', the Hermaphrodite,

> Which looks so sweet and gentle that it vexes
> The very soul that the soul is gone
> Which lifted from her limbs the veil of stone.

Here art is conceived as that which veils and obscures
the reality of the spirit.

---

[1] The lacuna is in the original text.

III

Another significant case of Shelley's use of symbolism is that which shows him as a transvaluer of the customary ethical values. He frequently takes as images of good things ordinarily associated with evil. He seems to do this partly through that sympathy with the outcast which was always strong in him, and was intensified by the social and legal injustice which he conceived himself to have undergone; partly—and this case is the converse of the first—through his fierce dislike of all stereotyped forms and images of morality. This dislike is in its turn connected with his belief that the division between good and evil, ugliness and beauty, is a thin one, and easily removable, were the heart of man once turned to the task. This latter aspect of Shelley's faith is discussed elsewhere in this volume. Here we can only instance a few of the symbols in which these convictions take form. The most important among these is, perhaps, the famous struggle between the eagle and the serpent at the beginning of *The Revolt of Islam.* This struggle had already furnished a simile of *Alastor*:

> As an eagle grasped
> In folds of the green serpent, feels her breast
> Burn with the poison, and precipitates
> Through night and day, tempest, and calm, and cloud,
> Frantic with dizzying anguish, her blind flight
> O'er the wide aery wilderness.

Here there is no sympathy with the serpent, nor any attempt to identify him with the principle of good: rather is he a malign thing distilling poison, which, as we shall see, is one of Shelley's recurrent symbols of evil. Furthermore, here it is he who vanquishes the eagle, and brings him to destruction. But in the First Canto of *The Revolt of Islam*, he is the eagle's victim, and after his terrific fight with him, he falls wounded into the sea, to be picked up and cherished by his rescuer in her bosom. It then appears, from the account given by her to the poet, that the serpent is the Morning Star, changed by his victorious foe, the Red Comet, 'from starry shape, beauteous and mild, to a dire snake, with man and beast unreconciled.' He is the principle of good, and the comet or fiend, 'whose name is legion', is the principle of 'Death, Decay, Earthquake and Blight and Madness pale, . . . Fear, Hatred, Faith and Tyranny.' The evil spirit assumes the eagle's shape since

> The darkness lingering o'er the dawn of things,
>   Was Evil's breath and life; this made him strong
> To soar aloft with overshadowing wings.

On the other hand, the great Spirit of Good in his changed form

>   did creep among
> The nations of mankind, and every tongue
> Cursed and blasphemed him as he passed; for none
> Knew good from evil.

Ever and anon the serpent and the eagle renew their fight, which symbolizes the strife of mankind against its oppressors, of freedom, justice and truth against 'Custom's hydra brood'. At the opening of the poem, the eagle has once more defeated his foe, but

>   The victor Fiend,
> Omnipotent of yore, now quails, and fears
> His triumph dearly won, which soon will lend
> An impulse swift and sure to his approaching end.

It is significant that in this poem evil is regarded as

a primary principle, not as a secondary accident or an accretion thwarting a single original principle of good. The relation of this conception to Shelley's general beliefs has been discussed elsewhere. It is further noteworthy that with Shelley the serpent is not a constant symbol of unrecognized beauty or goodness. The beauty of serpents is, indeed, frequently recognized: the snake in *Rosalind and Helen* floats on the 'dark and lucid flood in the light of his own loveliness': in the *Witch of Atlas* we light on 'the sly serpent, in the golden flame of his own volumes intervolved': and in *Adonais* 'the green lizard and the golden snake like unimprisoned flames out of their trance awake.' But elsewhere the serpent is, as commonly in all literatures, an emblem of evil: thus, in the breast of the Iberian priest in *The Revolt of Islam*

> Did hate and guile lie watchful, intertwined
> Twin serpents in one deep and winding nest.

A little later in the poem, snakes form part of the couch of torture on which the lovers are to perish. In *Marenghi* snakes and ill worms are numbered among 'things whose nature is at war with life': and in one of his posthumous lyrics Shelley says of music that

> It loosens the serpent which care has bound
> Upon my heart to stifle it.

Indeed, the whole tragedy of the Morning Star is that he has been doomed to assume a form which is commonly and naturally associated with the evil and the outcast. Shelley, in giving him this shape, wishes not only to awaken pity for him, but to exalt an object commonly regarded with contempt, and to show that it too has its part in the universal spirit, and

shall therefore share in the beneficence of the new order.
He states the same thought more explicitly, and in the
converse sense, in *Prometheus Unbound*:

> Common as light is love,
> And its familiar voice wearies not ever.
> Like the wide heaven, the all-sustaining air,
> It makes the reptile equal to the God:

and again, in *Epipsychidion*:

> The spirit of the worm beneath the sod
> In love and worship blends itself with God.

The meteor is another symbol which Shelley uses in
a different, if not an opposite, significance to the usual
one.   Traditionally the meteor had been regarded as
a thing of fear, portending disaster.   Because this is so,
there is no reason why Shelley, or any other poet,
should not portray it also as a thing of beauty; though
none other than he could have given the beauty the
peculiar unearthliness felt in the description of the
meteor in the *Fragments of an Unfinished Drama*:

> There the meteor lay,
> Panting forth light among the leaves and flowers,
> As if it lived, and was outworn with speed;
> Or that it loved, and passion made the pulse
> Of its bright life throb like an anxious heart
> Till it diffused itself, and all the chamber
> And walls seemed melted into emerald fire
> That burned not:

and again, in these lines of *Adonais*:

> The damp death
> Quenched its caress upon his icy lips;
> And as a dying meteor stains a wreath
> Of moonlight vapour, which the cold night clips,
> It flushed through his pale limbs, and passed to its
>   eclipse:

and yet again, in the still more unearthly and more
beautiful passage of *Marenghi*:

> And the marsh-meteors, like tame beasts, at night
>   Came licking with blue tongues his veinéd feet;
> And he would watch them, as, like spirits bright,
>   In many entangled figures quaint and sweet
> To some enchanted music they would dance—
> Until they vanished at the first moon-glance.

But with Shelley, apparently through a quite conscious
reversal of normal values, the meteor is not only beautiful but constantly beneficent. It is a kindly meteor
which shows each other's beauty to Laon and Cythna,

>   while the song
>   Of blasts, in which its blue hair quivering bent,
> Strewed strangest sounds the moving leaves among;
> A wondrous light, the sound as of a spirit's tongue.

Similarly 'long blue meteors cleansing the dull night'
are numbered by Earth in *Prometheus Unbound* with
'rainbow-skirted showers and odorous winds', and other
kindly influences of heaven: and again, as the Lady of
The Sensitive Plant walks in her garden of beauty

>   the meteors of that sublunar Heaven,
> Like the lamps of the air when Night walks forth,
> Laughed round her footsteps up from the Earth!

One of the very few instances which I find in Shelley
of this symbol's being used in a malign or sinister sense,
occurs in *The Sensitive Plant*: and here the meteors are
made evil at the close only by way of contrast with the
beautiful and kindly meteors of the beginning:

> And unctuous meteors from spray to spray
> Crept and flitted in broad noonday
> Unseen; every branch on which they alit
> By a venomous blight was burned and bit.

IV

We may pass to another case of Shelley's symbolism
—that in which he uses certain constantly recurring
images to express evil, as he sees it in the scheme ot
things. The words 'poison' and 'poisonous' occur
again and again throughout his writings, and, indeed,
became almost an obsession with him. Already in the
juvenile poems and *Queen Mab* Shelley has become
attached to the word, and we meet such phrases as

A balm was in the poison of the sting,

Commerce! beneath whose poison-breathing shade
No solitary virtue dares to spring,

the lot of human life
Which poisoned, body and soul, scarce drags the chain
That lengthens as it goes, and clanks behind,

the flesh
With putrid smoke poisoning the atmosphere,

that which lifts
His nature to the heaven of its pride,
Is bartered for the poison of his soul,

The wordy eloquence that lives
After the ruin of their hearts, can guild
The bitter poison of a nation's woe,

The iron rod of Penury still compels
Her wretched slave to bow the knee to wealth
And poison, with unprofitable toil.

Shelley's fondness for this symbol may be gathered
from the fact that the last three examples are taken
from a single page of *Queen Mab*. In this early, as in
his later, poetry, Shelley uses this image both in a physical and a spiritual sense. Into the first class fall
his references to 'self-destroying poisons in one cup'

'a weed whose shade is poison', the poison of night-shade, of a serpent's bite, of the drug through which a slave has lost his speech, of a robe of death—or

> Poison a snake in flowers, beneath the veil
> Of food and mirth hiding his mortal head.

Half physical, half allegorical are his references to fleshly food and wine as 'poisons'. Thus in *The Revolt of Islam* the happy time is forecast when men shall give up the eating of flesh and

> Avenging poisons shall have ceased
> To feed disease and fear and madness.

Concerning the great banquet of liberty, we are told that 'gore or poison none this festal did pollute.' But far more common and more significant are the cases in which Shelley uses 'poison' to express spiritual evil and corruption. This general use of the symbol may be seen in such lines as:

> A dream has power to poison sleep,

> Our Adonais has drunk poison,

> Thus all things were
> Transformed into the agony which I wore
> Even as a poisoned robe around my bosom's core,

> And how those seeds of hope might yet be sown
> Whose fruit is evil's mortal poison,

> Woman as the bond-slave dwells
> Of man, a slave, and life is poisoned in its wells,

> The dark fiend who, with his iron pen
> Dipped in scorn's fiery poison, makes his fame
> Enduring there.

The frequency with which Shelley employs this symbol in a spiritual context shows how intensely he felt both his own and the world's evil and misery, and how passionately he resented what he felt. We cannot,

I repeat, regard his constant repetition of the idea as a mere verbal echo or intellectual 'conceit': it corresponds to something deep-rooted in his soul—his poignant sense of the evil and suffering everywhere interwoven with the beauty of the world. The symbol, moreover, through its very intensity illustrates the sinister element in Shelley's imagination, which is never far to seek even in his most celestial flights. Yet even this symbol is used to express his belief that evil, deep-rooted though it is in the order of things, is still eradicable: for when the world has undergone the transforming spell of love,

Like passion's fruit the nightshade's tempting bane
Poisons no more the pleasure it bestows.

To Shelley, however, the most stubborn foes which love had to encounter in its task of regeneration were faith and tyranny. The faith which he hated, as is shown elsewhere in this volume, was not so much faith in Christ as faith in the Old Testament dispensation, and in historical Christianity. In *The Revolt of Islam* he uses the symbol of poison to express his scorn for

Traditions dark and old, whence evil creeds
Start forth, and whose dim shade a stream of poison
     feeds ;

and later in the same poem he assails

                    a faith
     Nursed by fear's dew of poison.

Elsewhere we are told that 'God is profuse of poisons', and in *Prometheus Unbound* the Titan, upbraiding the 'Monarch of Gods and Daemons', cries :

Heaven's winged hound, polluting from thy lips
His beak in poison not his own, tears up
My heart.

It is the same with kings as with gods. In the *Lines written among the Euganean Hills*, Shelley, looking down on the fair country around Padua, says in sorrow:

> And the sickle to the sword
> Lies unchanged, though many a lord,
> Like a weed whose shade is poison,
> Overgrows this region's foison,

and in the *Ode to Liberty* he says that the very sound of the name of king 'has poison in it'.

Another frequent image of evil with Shelley was the scorpion. In *Queen Mab* we are told that the slumbers of tormented man 'are but varied agonies, they prey like scorpions on the springs of life', and a few lines lower he is said to 'hug the scorpion that consumes him.' The tortured Laon in *The Revolt of Islam* says

> Thirst raged within me, like a scorpion's nest
> Built in mine entrails.

Later in the same poem the tyrant adds scorpions to his other instruments of torture, 'fire, pincers and the hook'. More significant are the cases in which Shelley uses the symbol to signify or illustrate some specific spiritual evil:

> The truths of their pure lips, that never die,
> Shall bind the scorpion falsehood with a wreath,
>   Of ever-living flame,
> Until the monster sting itself to death.

> Whilst Falsehood, tricked in Virtue's attributes,
> Long sanctified all deeds of vice and woe,
> Till done by her own venomous sting to death,
> She left the moral world without a law,
> No longer fettering Passion's fearless wing,
> Nor searing Reason with the brand of God.

> Want and Pest
> Were horrible, but one more fell doth rear,
> As in a hydra's swarming lair, its crest
> Eminent among those victims—even the Fear
> Of Hell: each girt by the hot atmosphere
> Of his blind agony, like a scorpion stung
> By his own rage upon his burning bier
> Of circling coals of fire.

There is a twofold significance in the use of this symbol, considered in relation to Shelley's general beliefs. In the first place, just as the scorpion stings itself, so does evil wound itself when it becomes active, since the stuff of all existence is one: in the second place—and this point becomes very clear in the second of the passages just quoted—evil, through the very law of its being, must eventually destroy itself after the scorpion's fashion, and disappear. This belief corresponds closely with Shelley's general teaching regarding evil, as explained elsewhere in this volume. It seems certain that he chose the scorpion for a symbol of evil largely because it possessed these last two attributes.

V

Another constantly recurring symbol of Shelley's is that of the Boat and the Stream. Here again it is, of course, possible to regard his references to the Boat as being merely reminiscences of a favourite pastime. As everyone remembers, boats and boating were always dear to his heart. We are told that when living at Cwm Elan, he would float a wooden boat, about a foot in length, down the swift mountain-streams, directing it from the bank with a pole, and keeping it from shipwreck on the rocks. Once, when short of paper, he used a banknote for a sail, and, on another occasion, a cat

became his unwilling passenger.   Throughout the greater part of his life he would sail paper boats on any
likely piece of water, and the pleasure he took in this
pastime is attested by several who knew him intimately.[1]
We even find him pursuing it in Henry Reveley's work-
shop:

> And in this bowl of quicksilver—for I
> Yield to the impulse of an infancy
> Outlasting manhood—I have made to float
> A rude idealism of a paper boat,
> A hollow screw with cogs.[2]

On one occasion, when watching one of these little

---

[1] 'He twisted a morsel of paper into a form that a lively fancy
might consider a likeness of a boat, and committing it to the water,
he anxiously watched the frail bark, which, if it was not soon
swamped by the faint winds and miniature waves, gradually
imbibed water through its porous sides and sank.   Sometimes,
however, the fairy vessel performed its little voyage and reached
the opposite shore of the puny ocean in safety.   It is astonishing
with what keen delight he engaged in this singular pursuit.   It is
not easy for an uninitiated spectator to bear with tolerable patience
the vast delay, on the brink of a wretched pond upon a bleak
common, and in the face of a cutting North-East wind, on returning
to dinner from a long walk at sunset on a cold winter's day ; nor
was it easy to be so harsh as to interfere with a harmless
gratification, that was evidently exquisite . . . So long as his
paper lasted, he remained riveted to the spot, fascinated by this
peculiar amusement.'   Hogg, *Life of Shelley*, vol. i, pp. 83, 84.

According to Peacock, one of Shelley's favourite resorts was
'a large pool of transparent water on a heath above Bracknell, with
determined borders, free from weeds, which admitted of launching
the miniature craft on the windward, and running round to receive
it on the leeward, side.   On the Serpentine he would sometimes
launch a boat constructed with more than usual care, and freighted
with half-pence.   He delighted to do this in the presence of boys
who would run round to meet it, and when it landed in safety, and
the boys scrambled for the prize, he had difficulty in restraining
himself from shouting as loudly as they did.'   *Memoirs of Shelley*,
Part II.   Cf. also Dowden, i. 269, 476; ii. 105, 334.

[2] *Letter to Maria Gisborne*, ll. 70–76.

craft running before the wind across a pond, he was inspired with a thought which now seems strangely prophetic. 'How much I should like', said he, 'that we could get into one of these boats and be shipwrecked—it would be a death to be more desired than any other.'

Shelley loved real boats no less than paper ones, and whenever he was near a sufficiently large piece of water, he rejoiced to sail or row in them. Twice before his last fatal voyage did this practice put his life in peril. Once, a storm came down and almost swamped the boat, 'keeled and clinker-built', in which he was sailing on the Lake of Geneva with Byron : again, when sailing on the Arno between Leghorn and Pisa with Henry Reveley and Williams, he was overturned in a gale, and was hauled ashore with difficulty by Reveley. We are told that at Marlow 'he would row up or down the river to some favourite spot and there let the boat drift while, as often on Lake Leman, he lay in the bottom gazing upward'. In life as in poetry, boats seem to have predisposed him toward mystical musing. In May, 1822, he took Jane Williams and her children for a row on the sea in his canoe, home-made of 'canvas and reeds, as light and small as possible'; and when they came to deep blue water, he gazed into it musingly and 'on a sudden raised his head and with brightening face exclaimed joyfully, " Now let us together solve the great mystery."' For him, at least, that mystery was solved a few weeks later by the tragic agency of another boat.

The material cause, then, of this symbol, as used by Shelley, may lie in his own practical experience. But it is impossible to account solely after this fashion for the imagery used by a great poet—especially when the great poet is also a great mystic. There is danger, on

the other hand, of our interpreting the symbol in too
strict or definite terms of metaphysical idea. We shall
best discover its meaning by looking into Shelley's main
uses of it.

We first encounter it in *Alastor*, where the wandering
and forlorn Poet finds ' a little shallop ' floating near the
shore where he has been wandering. It is at once
indicated that it is to be the means by which he will
find

> lone Death on the drear ocean's waste ;
> For well he knew that mighty Shadow loves
> The slimy caverns of the populous deep.

The boat is sped headlong over the sea by a hurricane.
Sea and sky are convulsed, but the Poet sits calm and
rejoicing amid the tumult. As the moon rises over the
cliffs of Caucasus, a cavern is seen yawning in the cliff
side, and the boat is whirled into it on the boiling torrent.
It is carried along a dark narrow chasm on a stream of
unfathomable depth, while overhead hang the gnarled
roots of mighty trees. The torrent sweeps on toward
a sheer abyss down which its volume falls, ' even to the
base of Caucasus.' Into the whirlpool at the edge of
this the boat ' passed shuddering ' : but instead of being
swept over the edge, it is carried into a smooth flowing
backwater, and speeds on, while the roar of the torrent
behind it mingles ' with the breeze murmuring in the
musical woods '. It is borne on, beneath the noonday
sun, through a forest,

> one vast mass
> Of mingling shade, whose brown magnificence
> A narrow vale embosoms.

The foliage grows thicker and more various and
gorgeous : and beneath it extend soft mossy lawns

'fragrant with perfumed herbs and eyed with blooms minute, yet beautiful'. In the heart of this pleasance is a dark and lovely glen, fragrant with 'a soul-dissolving odour', and guarded by Silence and Twilight. Beyond it lies 'a well, dark, gleaming, and of most translucent wave'. Here the Poet leaves the boat, and beholds his own sorrow-stricken face in the mirror of the well. A Spirit stands beside him and communes with him in the voice of

> undulating woods, and silent well,
> And leaping rivulet, and evening gloom
> Now deepening the dark shades:

and

> when his regard
> Was raised by intense pensiveness, . . . two eyes,
> Two starry eyes, hung in the gloom of thought,
> And seemed with their serene and azure smiles
> To beckon him.

He follows the course of the stream onwards beneath the shade of trees: death now gathers upon him: and as he advances and the stream broadens, the pleasant face of the valley changes, and it becomes a gloomy ravine, o'erhung with beetling precipices: while in the far distance are seen great seas and mountains, 'robed in the lustrous gloom of leaden-coloured even.' Amid this tract there is one nook, tranquil, smiling, and ivyclad, where none but the Poet had ever set foot: and here he is found by peace, and then by death.

In his quest the Poet, as the poem informs us, is led 'by love, or dream, or god, or mightier Death'. For him Death is the main guide: but the other forces here named are all at his call: and they are the forces swaying and kindling the spiritual force of which the Boat and the Stream are, in their different ways, the symbols.

As will be seen, in the other poems in which these two images occur the guiding force is generally not death: but it is almost invariably one of the other forces just named. In one sense the Stream in *Alastor* is the stream of human life, and of the Poet's own life. Thus he says :

> O stream!
> Whose source is inaccessibly profound,
> Whither do thy mysterious waters tend?
> Thou imagest my life. Thy darksome stillness,
> Thy dazzling waves, thy loud and hollow gulfs,
> Thy searchless fountain, and invisible course
> Have each their type in me.

But it also leads to ' Nature's dearest haunt, some bank, her cradle and his sepulchre ': and it represents some principle vaster than the mere human spirit, which enables the union between that spirit and cosmic nature to be realized, so that it is only stating part of the truth to identify the Stream absolutely with the poet's individual mind, as it has been identified by a modern critic. The Stream is not the poet's mind: it was in full flood before he reached it: but it flows *through* his mind or life and follows all its processes or stages. All the latter part of the poem turns on a conception fundamental with Shelley,—though elsewhere taking different form—that of the correspondence between the outer world and the inner—the correspondence emphasized in the description of the moon :

> Now upon the jagged hills
> It rests, and still as the divided frame
> Of the vast meteor sunk, the Poet's blood,
> That ever beat in mystic sympathy
> With nature's ebb and flow, grew feebler still.

In the lines preceding this passage Shelley speaks of

'the stream of thought', and refers to it as being 'calmly fed' by 'the influxes of sense and his own being unalloyed by pain'. The subjective thought here, as the repeated symbol of the Stream shows, is part of that vaster thought which in Shelley's view pulsed through all things and connected the universal mind with the particular. It should be noticed that in *Mont Blanc*, where the conception of this unity finds its supreme expression, Shelley once more uses the symbol of the Stream, which he regards as flowing *through* the individual mind. This passage is of great importance for the understanding of his general use of this image:

> The everlasting universe of things
> Flows through the mind, and rolls its rapid waves,
> Now dark,—now glittering—now reflecting gloom—
> Now lending splendour, where from secret springs
> The source of human thought its tribute brings
> Of waters,—with a sound but half its own,
> Such as a feeble brook will oft assume
> In the wild woods, among the mountains lone,
> Where waterfalls around it leap for ever,
> Where woods and winds contend, and a vast river
> Over its rocks ceaselessly bursts and raves.

If the Stream is the universal stream of thought which flows through the universe and all human life, the Boat is the individual human soul which is received by that stream and swept along toward its spiritual consummation. This identification seems to be assured by the instances under discussion, as well as by the numerous other appearances of the symbol throughout Shelley's poetry. It is used in this sense in Asia's song at the end of the Second Act of the *Prometheus*:

> My soul is an enchanted boat,
> Which, like a sleeping swan, doth float
> Upon the silver waves of thy sweet singing.

As is shown elsewhere, all the imagery of this song corresponds with the imagery of the voyage given in *Alastor* and *The Revolt of Islam*. As the Boat is admittedly the human soul in the Song, it is presumably also this in the longer poems. It has the same meaning in the *Fragment to One Singing*, where the Stream is again the stream of song, and the voyage, as far as it is described, corresponds with the other voyages of our discussion :

My spirit like a charmed bark doth swim
    Upon the liquid waves of thy sweet singing,
Far far away into the regions dim
    Of rapture—as a boat, with swift sails winging
  Its way adown some many-winding river,
Speeds through dark forests o'er the waters swinging.

And at the end of *Adonais* the bark is again stated to be the human soul :

The breath whose might I have invoked in song
Descends on me ; my spirit's bark is driven,
Far from the shore, far from the trembling throng
Whose sails were never to the tempest given.

In *Alastor*, 'love, or dream, or god, or mightier death' are cited as the forces which may launch the human soul upon the universal stream of Imagination in its supreme quest. Of the particular quest which is the subject of this poem death is the benign consummation : but the Poet in his journey towards death has penetrated the depths of Nature, and has understood her kinship with his own soul : and he has also realized his vision of human love through the eyes of his beloved. Death, however, is the main and ultimate goal of his striving. In *The Revolt of Islam* the goal is love—love between man and woman, and the love of both for their kind.

At the beginning of the poem occurs an isolated simile
which shows how strong a hold the symbols of the
Boat and Stream had at this time obtained upon
Shelley's mind. He is describing how the storm is
sweeping down toward him the interlocked shapes of
the Eagle and the Snake, which in the distance at first
appear to be a single winged Form :

> Even like a bark, which from a chasm of mountains
>   Dark, vast, and overhanging, on a river
> Which there collects the strength of all its fountains,
>   Comes forth, whilst with the speed its frame doth
>   quiver,
>   Sails, oars, and stream, tending to one endeavour ;
> So, from that chasm of light a wingèd Form
>   On all the winds of heaven approaching ever
> Floated, dilating as it came : the storm
> Pursued it with fierce blasts, and lightnings swift and
>   warm.

Later in the First Canto the Poet, after watching the
struggle between the Eagle and the Serpent, is borne
away with the Woman who had rescued the serpent in

> A boat of rare device, which had no sail
> But its own curvèd prow of thin moonstone.

They speed over the sea while the Woman tells the
story of the Morning Star and of her own life, till they
come to the wondrous Temple where

>   there sate on many a sapphire throne,
>   The Great, who had departed from mankind,
> A mighty Senate,

—the temple in which Cythna is to tell the tale of herself
and Laon. Here, perhaps, the symbolism of the Boat
is less definite than it had been in *Alastor*. I think,
however, that it is meant to be something more than
a mere piece of the machinery of fancy, devised to

convey the Poet from the scene of the struggle : and
it is significant that it is sped to its goal by

> those gentlest winds which are not known
> To breathe, but by the steady speed alone
> With which it cleaves the sparkling sea.

Surely we have here another vision of the human soul
sped forth on the winds of the spirit in search this time
not of death, but of love—the love of humankind
which is the main theme of the poem, and whose temple
is the goal of the mystic voyage. At the end of the
poem, after the lovers have undergone death by torment
for the love of humanity, their spirits are once more
swept by a 'charmèd boat' toward the same fair haven.
The Boat is, in all essentials, the Boat of *Alastor* and of
the earlier episode of *The Revolt*:

> The boat was one curved shell of hollow pearl,
>   Almost translucent with the light divine
> Of her within ; the prow and stern did curl
>   Hornèd on high, like the young moon supine,
>   When o'er dim twilight mountains dark with pine,
> It floats upon the sunset's sea of beams,
>   Whose golden waves in many a purple line
> Fade fast, till borne on sunlight's ebbing streams,
> Dilating, on earth's verge the sunken meteor gleams.

This time, however, the 'divine canoe' has a captain or
pilot—a 'plumèd Seraph . . . a child with silver-shining
wings', the spirit, apparently, of the child who earlier
in the poem had been dancing innocently before the
fallen tyrant, and who, when the tyrant regains power,
pleads vainly before him for Laon's life. Cythna claims
her as her own child, and she becomes the guiding spirit
of the quest. The Boat, as in *Alastor*, is swept along
a swift stream through varied and wondrous scenes of

beauty, now traversing whirlpools iridescent with bright
sunshine, now passing melodious waters falling among
flowerclad rocks, now threading her way o'er a vast
lake studded with green islands beneath the moonlight's
'holier day'. Onward the voyagers speed past smiling
meadows and vast mountains, and through wide and
vaulted caves; but though the scenes traversed are
often wild and majestic, they are never gloomy and
terrible as in *Alastor*: and to gladden the travellers'
sight

> from their deep
> And dark-green chasms, shades beautiful and
> white,
> Amid sweet sounds across our path would sweep,
> Like swift and lovely dreams that walk the waves
> of sleep.

For the voyage is now one of hope and joy, not, as in
Alastor, one in which death is the supreme quest and
mercy. In *The Revolt of Islam* death has been faced
and conquered, and it is seen that when he has done
his worst he is powerless to destroy the achievement of
the human spirit :

> We did know,
> That virtue, though obscured on Earth, not less
> Survives all mortal change in lasting loveliness.

In this poem, the Boat and the Stream are symbols of
the human soul sweeping on beyond the grave toward
that unity in Love which is the consummation of the
universal spirit :

> That Light whose smile kindles the Universe,
> That Beauty in which all things work and move,
> That Benediction which the eclipsing Curse
> Of birth can quench not, that sustaining Love

> Which through the web of being blindly wove
> By man and beast and earth and air and sea,
> Burns bright or dim, as each are mirrors of
> The fire for which all thirst.

Imagination has won its supreme triumph : and its spirit
is the seraph child, just as in *The Witch of Atlas* the
spirit of Fancy accompanying the voyagers along the
Stream is the more elvish and less sublime hermaphrodite. It is significant that this being has not a heavenly
and independent existence like the Seraph's, but is
a shape fashioned by the Witch's own art :

> Then by strange art she kneaded fire and snow
>   Together, tempering the repugnant mass
> With liquid love—all things together grow
>   Through which the harmony of love can pass ;
> And a fair Shape out of her hands did flow—
>   A living Image, which did far surpass
> In beauty that bright shape of vital stone
> Which drew the heart out of Pygmalion.

The Seraph, moreover, had powers of revelation and
control, and was the guide of the voyagers as well as
their comrade : the Hermaphrodite is the servant of the
Witch, and remains passive till she calls it into life, and
bids it perform her hests :

> And ever as she went, the Image lay
>   With folded wings and unawakened eyes ;
> And o'er its gentle countenance did play
>   The busy dreams, as thick as summer flies.

This particular distinction is surely significant of the
general distinction between the Witch's voyage and the
voyages in *Alastor* and *The Revolt of Islam*. The
Hermaphrodite corresponds to an inferior faculty of the
soul to that represented by the Seraph. Its changes
follow the bright play of the Witch's fancy, and it fulfils
her whims instead of guiding her soul. Similarly,

in *The Witch of Atlas*, the Stream of spirit issues forth,
and along it are borne the Witch and her bark : but it
does not sweep her imperiously on to the supreme
realization of love or death, but rather gives her fancy
its freedom, and allows it to play half elvishly, half
beneficently over the order of Nature, now 'circling the
image of a shooting star', now riding 'singing through
the shoreless air', or gliding 'adown old Nilus', and
again visiting sleeping mortals, inspiring the good and
beautiful with fair dreams, and turning the sinister
imaginings of the evil sleepers to nought. But though
her influence is beneficent, she regards what she sees
but lightly and in sport, and does not view human
injustice and wrong with the passionate resentment
which inspires Laon and Cythna. When she saw

> all the code of Custom's lawless law
> Written upon the brows of old and young :
> ' This', said the wizard maiden, 'is the strife
> Which stirs the liquid surface of man's life.'

And little did the sight disturb her soul.

This lack of the highest imaginative sympathy in the
Witch corresponds closely with the symbolism of the
poem, and with the marked differences between it and
the symbolism of its predecessors : and it is also closely
connected with the Witch's lack of passion—she was
' like a sexless bee tasting all blossoms and confined to
none '—since, in Shelley's view, passion was essential to
all the highest forms of spiritual self-realization.

Just as the Witch creates the hermaphrodite, so does
she inspire the Boat with its moving force :

> This boat she moored upon her fount, and lit
> A living spirit within all its frame,
> Breathing the soul of swiftness into it.

If the Boat in Shelley's poetry generally represents, as I
believe it does, the human soul, in this case that soul is
sped forth on its quest by the mere conscious and
personal impulse of Fancy, instead of being impelled, as
in *Alastor* and *The Revolt of Islam*, through Imagination
or some mystic force in which it participates, but which
is far mightier than itself. Yet the first part of the
Witch's voyage lies through scenes of grandeur and
beauty closely resembling those of the voyages in the
earlier poems :

> And down the streams which clove those mountains
>   vast,
>   Around their inland islets, and amid
> The panther-peopled forests, whose shade cast
>   Darkness and odours, and a pleasure hid
> In melancholy gloom, the pinnace passed ;
>   By many a star-surrounded pyramid
> Of icy crag cleaving the purple sky,
> And caverns yawning round unfathomably.

Later, however, the swift clear progress of the voyage,
which in the previous poems leads direct to a sublime
consummation, is dissolved in the elvishness which
gives *The Witch of Atlas* its peculiar and exquisite
glamour :

> These were tame pleasures ; she would often climb
>   The steepest ladder of the crudded rack
> Up to some beakèd cape of cloud sublime,
>   And like Arion on the dolphin's back
> Ride singing through the shoreless air ;—oft-time
>   Following the serpent lightning's winding track,
> She ran upon the platforms of the wind,
> And laughed to hear the fire-balls roar behind.

In the Song of Asia, to which we have already referred,
there recur not only the Boat and the Stream, but also

the guardian spirit, and the varied and beautiful imagery
of the voyage.   The Stream is music, and it carries the
Boat towards 'realms where the air we breathe is love'.
In this twofôld fact we are doubtless intended to realize
once more the conception, so constant in Shelley, of the
close kinship, amounting even to unity, which exists
between the highest artistic and the highest ethical
expressions of the human spirit.   This unity or kinship
we find again in *Prometheus Unbound* in the songs of
the first Four Spirits in the First Act.   In the Song,
as in *Alastor*, the Stream, though it is more than life,
flows through life, whose different phases appear in
succession in the scenery of its banks.   Here, it will be
noted, the course of life is threaded backwards toward
the state of love and innocence beyond birth, the
conception being analogous to the one embodied in
Wordsworth's *Immortality Ode* :

> We have passed Age's icy caves,
> And Manhood's dark and tossing waves,
> And Youth's smooth ocean, smiling to betray:
> Beyond the glassy gulfs we flee
> Of shadow-peopled Infancy,
> Through Death and Birth, to a diviner day;
> A paradise of vaulted bowers,
> Lit by downward-gazing flowers,
> And watery paths that wind between
> Wildernesses calm and green,
> Peopled by shapes too bright to see,
> And rest, having beheld; somewhat like thee;
> Which walk upon the sea, and chant melodiously!

Here, then, we have the converse of the last scene
in *The Revolt of Islam*, where the human spirit voyages
to its consummation after death.   The conception of an
antenatal state of happiness is fairly common in Shelley.

It appears toward the conclusion of *Queen Mab*, again in
relation to the Stream of universal mind:

> For birth and life and death, and that strange state
> Before the naked soul has found its home,
> All tend to perfect happiness, and urge
> The restless wheels of being on their way,
> Whose flashing spokes, instinct with infinite life,
> Bicker and burn to gain their destined goal:
> For birth but wakes the spirit to the sense
> Of outward shows, whose unexperienced shape
> New modes of passion to its frame may lend.

There is an echo of the same idea in the passage
of *Epipsychidion*, in which Shelley, after describing the
exquisite sights and sounds of the island, adds:

> And every motion, odour, beam, and tone,
> With that deep music is in unison:
> Which is a soul within the soul—they seem
> Like echoes of an antenatal dream.

In *Lines written in the Euganean Hills*, Shelley once
more uses the symbol of the Boat to express the human
soul.   Here the significance of the image is more
obvious and less transcendental than in the previous
cases.   The poem opens with the vision of a mariner
tempest-driven in fear and peril

> O'er the unreposing wave
> To the haven of the grave.

At the end of the poem the voyage of the Poet's bark
ends in the realization of mundane, if idyllic, happiness.
Some of the Spirits which 'float and flee' over 'the sea
of Life and Agony', are imagined as waiting

> For my bark, to pilot it
> To some calm and blooming cove,
> Where for me, and those I love,
> May a windless bower be built,
> Far from passion, pain, and guilt,

In a dell mid lawny hills,
Which the wild sea-murmur fills,
And soft sunshine, and the sound
Of old forests echoing round,
And the light and smell divine
Of all flowers that breathe and shine.

VI

Attention has often been drawn to the great attraction
possessed for Shelley by the moon, and to the constant
references made throughout his poetry to its beauty and
influence.   In one of the essays in his *Ideas of Good and
Evil* Mr. W. B. Yeats has discussed this aspect of
Shelley's symbolism eloquently, and with insight.[1]
Here I only wish to emphasize the part played by the
moon in the particular variety of Shelley's imagery
which we have just been discussing.   The rise of the
moon enables the Poet of *Alastor* to see the cavern
in the cliffs of Caucasus into which his shallop is swept
by the torrent.   After he has pursued his voyage through
the changes of the night and of the next day, he
approaches the scene of his death at the hour when

The dim and hornèd moon hung low, and poured
A sea of lustre on the horizon's verge
That overflowed its mountains.

We have seen that his life fails as the moon sinks,
and that when it sets he dies.   Again, the Boat at
the beginning of *The Revolt of Islam* has a 'curvèd prow
of thin moonstone', sways 'like the moon's shade'
among the stars reflected on the water, and makes

[1] The reader is referred to the same essay for an analysis of the
symbolism of the Boat, the Stream, and the Cave which differs
considerably from the present analysis.

a great part of its voyage beneath the rising moon. The Temple of its quest has a roof of moonstone, and is adorned within

> with starry shapes between,
> And hornèd moons, and meteors strange and fair.

The symbol of the moon recurs in the description of the Boat in which the spirits of Laon and Cythna make their final voyage. The prow and stern of this

> did curl
> Hornèd on high, like the young moon supine,
> When o'er dim twilight mountains dark with pine,
> It floats upon the sunset's sea of beams;

and it is not without significance that the symbol of the moon which runs through the poem takes shape in its last lines, and is there used of the Boat as it nears the Temple of the Spirit:

> on the sound
> Which issued thence, drawn nearer and more near,
> Like the swift moon this glorious earth around,
> The charmèd boat approached, and there its haven found.

It is appropriate that the poem should end in an image suggested by the planet always dear to Shelley—the planet of magic and calm and hope.

THE SINISTER IN SHELLEY

I

It is to be hoped that the day is long past when any one who writes an essay with this title may run the risk of being classed with Shelley's detractors. To-day the celestial strain in his life is in as little danger of being overlooked as the celestial strain in his poetry: and whatever other elements may emerge, there can be no manner of doubt that beauty and goodness formed the positive element in his life and song. It must be obvious, however, to the most trivial student of him that there were other things in his nature besides light and ecstasy and aspiration. It is the object of the present essay to disengage these, to show that there was that in his poetry which puts him in touch rather with Poe and Baudelaire than with his beloved Sophocles and Plato, and that this literary quality is inseparably connected with a certain strain in his character, as manifested in the everyday relations of his life. For the sake of clearness and proportion, however, it will be convenient to glance for a moment at the fairer and more obvious side of the medal. The evidence here is copious and familiar : it is forthcoming from every man and woman who knew him well. Even as a child of six he was inspired with the passion of protection, and, so his sister tells us, wished to purchase and educate a diminutive 'tumbler who came to the back door to display her wonderful feats'. At Eton his love of his kind was quickened by the respective messages—as he then understood them—of Godwin and Condorcet.   Hogg tells us that when he was at Oxford, 'the heart of the young virgin who has never crossed her father's threshold to encounter the rude world could not be more susceptible of all the sweet domestic charities than his.'   The same laughing yet not unloving onlooker draws a delightful picture of Shelley succouring with warm milk, hastily procured from a neighbouring cottage, a peasant girl whom he had found faint with cold and hunger on an Oxford hillside.   A similar picture—perhaps even a more touching one—of Shelley as saviour·is given in Leigh Hunt's *Autobiography*.

Instances of his benevolence to man and beast might be multiplied almost to infinity: sometimes it took the quaint form of ordering his manservant, Harry, to [1] 'purchase crayfish of the men who brought them through the streets, and bear them back to their lurking places in the Thames'.   And we are told that near the very end, at Lerici, 'wherever there was sickness in the house, there would he be found nursing and advising.' Perhaps one would most fitly symbolize Shelley as man were one to show him kneeling before the sick, or bearing some starving woman out of darkness and despair into light and warmth and charity.

His generosity in money matters to friends and strangers is even better known.   The youth who had lavished all his spare money on the needy peasants as he rode the rounds of his father's estate, in manhood refused himself luxuries and even necessary food, so that he might assist the needy men of letters who were his friends.   Not the least remarkable episode in his

---

[1] Dowden, *Life of Shelley*, ii. 123.

life is that in which Godwin, while treating Shelley
with hostility and contempt as the vulgar seducer of his
daughter, accepts the £1,000 which he had promised him
as a free gift, and duns him remorselessly for the balance
of £200. Altogether, Godwin appears to have received
from Shelley no less a sum than £5,000. On the needy
Peacock he settled an annuity of £100, while he gave
substantial sums of money to Leigh Hunt, and also
became his bond to Byron for a loan of £200. As is
generally the case with the open-handed, his bounty
soon came to be taken as a matter of course, and we
find Mrs. Gisborne's son-in-law, Henry Reveley, obtain-
ing money from him for the construction of his steam-
boat, and Charles Clairmont, Godwin's stepson, begging
him for an allowance so that he might marry the charming Mlle. Jeanne Morel, and settle down as 'a hardy
campagnard' on 'a little métairie' in the Pyrenees.

One of the most striking testimonies to the beauty of
Shelley's character was the love and admiration which
he inspired in all his friends, male or female. 'The
moment he entered a house,' says Hogg, 'he inspired
the most lively interest in every woman in the family.'
He was cherished as 'the apple of beauty's eye'. His
conversation held them spellbound, though like Sterne's
Yorick in the ruffle-shop of the fair *grisette*, they were
evidently thinking more of the speaker than of the thing
spoken, for 'none of them could ever remember what he
had been talking about'. Men regarded him with an
enthusiasm equally intense, though possibly more dis-
criminating; and the spiritual beauty of his nature is
attested not only by impressionable fellow poets like
Leigh Hunt, but by roving adventurers like Trelawny,
by Byron the libertine, by Peacock of the cynic brain,

and even by Medwin of the leaden soul. The most radiant picture we possess of him during the last days of his life is that supplied by Trelawny, who describes how he himself ran shouting with joy from the bitter and sinister company of Byron, to the 'hospitable and cheerful abode of the Shelleys', where he 'found those sympathies and sentiments which the Pilgrim denounced as illusions believed in as the only realities'. He continues: 'To form a just idea of his poetry, you should have witnessed his daily life. If his glorious conception of Gods and men constituted an atheist, I am afraid all that listened were little better. . . . The truth was, Shelley loved everything better than himself. Self-preservation is, they say, the first law of Nature; with him it was the last; and the only pain he ever gave his friends rose from the utter indifference with which he treated everything concerning himself.' Byron described him as 'the best and most benevolent of men', and said that every man he had ever met was a beast beside Shelley. Peacock, as we shall see, clearly recognized the less ingenuous principle in Shelley ; yet he too bears testimony, in his colder fashion, to the beauty and good-ness of his nature.

If we turn from his life to his work it would seem super-fluous to follow his passionate love of his kind through his prose and poetry, from *Queen Mab* and *The Address to the Irish People*, through the *Revolt of Islam* and *Prometheus Unbound*, to *Hellas* and *The Triumph of Life*. The growth and manifestations of that love have been described in another essay of this volume. Here again, no one can fail to recognize in this impulse the main current of his soul, which beat imperiously against the flood-gates of song, threw them apart, and streamed

forth in exultant lyric ecstasy.   It is sufficient for our
present purpose to say that, together with his passion
for freedom and hatred of oppression, there recur
throughout all his early work a repudiation of force as
the antidote to tyranny, and throughout all his work,
from beginning to end, a vehement assertion that the
hatred of evil qualities must not mean the hatred of evil
men.   Personal rancour of this kind, whether in himself
or others, he passionately denounced and repudiated as
running counter to the master-principle of all existence,
Love.   The distinction is stated clearly in his *Lines to
a Reviewer*, beginning

> Alas, good friend, what profit can you see
> In hating such a hateless thing as me?
> There is no sport in hate where all the rage
> Is on one side:

and it reappears in his *Lines to a Critic*:

> Honey from silk-worms who can gather
>   Or silk from the yellow bee?
> The grass may grow in winter weather
>   As soon as hate in me.
>   .   .   .   .
> A passion like the one I prove
> Cannot divided be.
> I hate thy want of truth and love—
> How can I then hate thee?

It will be one object of this essay to inquire whether
such a view of the matter as has been hitherto developed
accounts completely for Shelley's life and work, or
whether, on the other hand, the very intensity of his
idealism did not result on occasions in a reaction of
sinister imagining and emotion.

II

It is the same, then, with Shelley when we pass from his conduct and general thought to the moods expressed in his greatest poetry—that lyric effluence of light and purity by which we know and love him best. He is best remembered by such passages as Asia's long and exquisite speech in the second act of *Prometheus Unbound*, or *Life of Life*, or the soaring close of *Epipsychidion*, or that perfect flower piece, *The Question*, or *Mutability*, or *Rarely, rarely, comest thou.* The unearthliness which is the distinctive note of all his higher poetry is here celestial, and this not less in the passages of despair than in those of ecstasy. The same glory is upon him when he stands 'at noon upon the peak of Heaven', as when, in *Prince Athanase*, he passes through the 'Night of the Soul', or, remaining with his kind, becomes the 'nerve o'er which do creep the else unfelt oppressions of this earth'. It flames forth in such an ecstasy of joy as this:

Her voice is hovering o'er my soul—it lingers
    O'ershadowing it with soft and lulling wings,
The blood and life within those snowy fingers
    Teach witchcraft to the instrumental strings.
My brain is wild, my breath comes quick—
    The blood is listening in my frame,
And thronging shadows, fast and thick,
    Fall on my overflowing eyes;
My heart is quivering like a flame;
    As morning dew, that in the sunbeam dies,
    I am dissolved in these consuming ecstasies.

But it is hardly less strong and lovely in the despairing

Swifter far than summer's flight—
Swifter far than youth's delight—
Swifter far than happy night,
    Art thou come and gone—

As the earth when leaves are dead,
As the night when sleep is sped,
As the heart when joy is fled,
   I am left lone, alone.

The swallow summer comes again—
The owlet night resumes her reign—
But the wild-swan youth is fain
   To fly with thee, false as thou.—
My heart each day desires the morrow;
Sleep itself is turned to sorrow;
Vainly would my winter borrow
   Sunny leaves from any bough.

In both of these passages, opposite as is their mood, there is a common element of beauty and feeling, and even of rhythm.   Innumerable instances of the same quality might be cited.   In all of these places Shelley walks with an angel, even though it be in darkness— with the angel who was his true and most constant guardian.   There were other times when he could walk in darkness, and in daylight too, in the grip of a devil of the pit.   For our present purpose, the antithesis is not the easy one between joy and gloom, ecstasy and despair.   In the darkest of the passages just cited there is no touch of what he himself calls the 'daemonic': conversely, there is another beauty in Shelley, and a very real one, suffused by no gleam of celestial light.   So far we have not met the sinister in him : and it is the sinister we seek.

Before looking to Shelley's poetry for this, it will be helpful to glance at certain aspects of his life, with which the sinister in his work would seem to be inseparably connected.   The first of these concerns his relations toward reality and truth.   Considered in this regard, Shelley's psychological condition is interesting and obscure.   From his earliest childhood he had delighted in pretence and mystification.   He would play at devils with his sisters : [1]—' Sometimes Bysshe and his sisters became themselves a crew of supernatural monsters : the little girls, in strange garbs, were fiends, Bysshe, the great devil, bearing along the passage to the back door a fire-stove flaming with his infernal liquids. When Bysshe one day set a fagot-stack on fire, the excuse was a charming one—he did so that he might have a little hell of his own.' At other times he would tell his sisters how a hoary alchemist lived in a secret chamber of their house, and how a Great Tortoise might be found in Warnham Pond, and a ' Great Old Snake ' in the gardens of Field Place. On another occasion,[2] ' he gave the most minute details of a visit he had paid to some ladies with whom he was acquainted at our village. He described their reception of him, their occupations, and the wandering in their pretty garden—all which was sportive invention, motiveless except for the pleasure of a jest.' None of these instances is in any way abnormal as an expression of boyish fancy, though that fancy with Shelley passes easily into a less normal form of deception which was to grow upon him ·a little later in life. At this age, his friend Halliday informs us, he would tell 'marvellous stories of fairyland and apparitions of spirits beyond the grave '. This pleasant variety of deception might be further illustrated, but it is more to our purpose to pass to those instances in which Shelley's imagination leaves the strand of make-believe, and plays strange tricks with the facts of common life. His youthful conviction, or pretence of conviction, that he had overheard his father consulting about sending him to a private madhouse, may be regarded by us, as it was

[1] Dowden, i. 10.
[2] Hellen Shelley, quoted by Hogg and Dowden.

regarded by Hogg, as the result of the fever from which he was suffering at the time. But it was no fever known to medical science which afterwards caused him to give Godwin a totally unveracious account of his expulsion from Eton, and from Oxford,[1] and further to inform him that his father wanted to drive him through poverty into accepting a commission in some remote regiment, and, during his absence, to have him prosecuted and outlawed for his atheistical pamphlet, so that the estate might devolve upon his younger brother. Hogg disbelieved, and we too may disbelieve, his story that shortly before he came to Oxford he had taken poison for the love of a young lady, but that his stomach had rejected it, leaving him a ruined constitution as the price of life. Hogg tells us that it was a main rule of conduct with him to make a mystery of everything: to 'treat as a profound secret matters manifest, patent, and fully known to everybody'. The converse of this quality is evident in the strange business of the Tanyrallt shooting case. According to Shelley, this was a deliberate attempt to murder him, made by a man who entered his rooms late at night, fired at him, and then knocked him down, after Shelley had missed fire with his first pistol. After a struggle, Shelley fired his second pistol, and the man fled, returning again three hours later to thrust his arm through the glass and fire at Shelley again. After some more struggling, he broke away and vanished, just as the servant, Daniel Hill, entered the room.[2] Next morning Shelley, according to Medwin, swore

---

[1] Hogg's *Life of Shelley*, vol. ii, chap. 3.

[2] This account of the affair is the one given by Harriet in a letter to Hookham immediately after its alleged occurrence. It differs considerably from the version supplied by Medwin, and subsequently by Shelley himself.

to the occurrence in the presence of the magistrate, Mr. Madocks. There seems no reason for believing Shelley's account of the matter, and there are many strong reasons for disbelieving it. In the first place he seems to have met delusion or deception half way : for, contrary to his wont, he loaded his pistols before retiring to bed, though he never alleged, nor appears to have had, any just cause for doing so. Secondly, there were no footmarks to be found on certain portions of the soaking wet lawn which the assassin must have crossed to get to the scene of action. Thirdly, the bullet which Shelley alleged to have been fired at him by the assassin *from* the window, and to have perforated his night dress, was afterwards found lodged in the wainscoting in such a position that it must have been fired *towards* the window. This alleged outrage has been successively fathered on the unfortunate Leeson, on Elizabeth Hitchener's father, and on an irate sheep-farmer. The special pleading of certain writers [1] has recently been directed to showing that it actually took place. One wonders whether these authorities wish us also to admit the reality of the ghost, or devil, which, so Shelley told Mrs. Williams, he had seen leaning against a tree just after the occurrence. It is significant that Shelley's account of the affair was utterly disbelieved in the locality at the time, and was also disbelieved by the friends who knew him best, including the Newtons, Williams of Tremadoc, Peacock, Hogg, and, eventually, Hookham. Hogg, in particular, remarks : ' Persons acquainted with the localities and with the circumstances, and who had carefully investigated the matter, were unanimous in the opinion that no such

---

[1] e. g. Miss Margaret L. Croft, *The Century Magazine*, October, 1905.

attempt was ever made. I never met with any person who believed in it.' Features of the case not actually fatal to Shelley's account, but suspicious when considered with the rest, are the intruder's suddenly having vanished in the instant that Daniel entered the room, and the melodramatic ring of the words he addressed to Shelley at his first parting, 'By God, I will be revenged! I will murder your wife! I will ravish your sister! By God! I will be revenged!'

This occurrence, in itself of no particular importance, has been related at length for its striking bearing on the condition of Shelley's mind. Was he on this evening, as Medwin hints, the victim of a hallucination caused by the wildness of the scenery, the loneliness of the spot, his want of wholesome reading, and an imagined enemy? Did he in fact visualize the would-be assassin, as Blake on a celebrated occasion visualized the ghost of a flea? Or did he himself disbelieve in his own account, and merely wish, not necessarily for the interested reasons advanced by Leeson, to make his friends believe in it? Are we to assume delusion or deception, or a mixture of both—semi-delusion, in fact? Speculation on this point remains obscure and vast. But whichever view we adopt, his relation to the world of reality was here apparently quite abnormal.

Deception of a quite conscious kind seems apparent in the curious story related by Shelley to the sceptical Peacock concerning the visit paid him by Williams of Tremadoc shortly before his departure from England in 1816. According to Shelley, Williams called on him to warn him of a plot laid by his father and uncle to place him under restraint. This, as has just been noticed, was an old obsession of Shelley's, and his recurrence to it might in itself have aroused suspicion in Peacock's mind. But apart from this, when he told his tale to Peacock, he alleged that he had walked back with Williams as far as Egham, and pointed to the hat he was holding in his hand as confirmation of his story. Peacock, however, noticed that the hat was not Shelley's, but his own, which Shelley had evidently taken up by mistake immediately before entering the room. He made Shelley put it on, and it went over his face down to the chin. Peacock's suspicions were now aroused ; it was clearly impossible that Shelley could have walked for miles in that hat without discovering his mistake. Shelley, noticing his scepticism, offered to walk with him to London on the next day, promising him that Williams would be found at the Turk's Head. On the way, Shelley changed his mind, saying that on reconsidering the matter he thought Williams would probably not be found there after all. Peacock said he thought this very likely. Shelley, piqued, declared that Williams had brought him a diamond necklace, and offered to show it to Peacock. Peacock replied that this would prove nothing but that he had a diamond necklace to show. It was Peacock's firm conviction that Williams had never called on Shelley at all : and whether we consider this story on its own merits, or with reference to what we know of Shelley's character, it is difficult not to share Peacock's view.

Here again the matter is quite unimportant, except in so far as it illustrates the peculiar working of Shelley's mind ; and in this case one is forced to conclude that his delusion had in it a conscious element, or was at best, to use Peacock's appropriate term, a ' semi-delusion '. Most people who have had much to do with boys must

have encountered such instances of imaginative misre-
presentation.   To the same period as this occurrence
belongs the visit said by Shelley to have been paid him
by the married woman, 'young, handsome, and of noble
connexions', who visited him before he left England,
and told him that her admiration for him had been
awakened by *Queen Mab*, and had rapidly ripened into
devotion.   She offered to sacrifice everything for him
and follow him through the world.   He gently refused
her request, but some three years later, so he declared,
she reappeared in Naples, having followed him in secret
through all his wanderings.   This story was believed by
Medwin, and to some extent corroborated by Claire
Clairmont.   Byron, however, who knew Shelley well,
flatly disbelieved it, just as Peacock disbelieved Shelley's
story that during 1820 an English officer in the
Portuguese service had felled him to the ground in the
Pisa post office, exclaiming :   'What, are you that
damned atheist, Shelley ? '

The ambiguity of Shelley's nature, and the two
distinct elements of conscious purpose and sheer
hallucination noticeable in his stories, may be illustrated
by two separate phenomena, relating to his physical
health, which are recorded by Hogg.   He possessed
a habit of inventing a delicate and dangerous condition
of health for himself, including 'spasms, consumption,
burstings of blood vessels, veins and arteries' when he
wished to find an excuse for some desired course
of action : but imagination—here his useful servant
—was to take a whimsical revenge on him when freed
from his conscious control.   Shelley once sat in a stage
coach opposite a woman whose legs were abnormally
swollen by what he considered to be elephantiasis.   He

had recently been reading an account of this illness in a medical treatise, and it was an easy step to imagine that he had caught it from the fat woman dozing opposite. This preyed so on his nerves that he subjected himself to examination by a skilful surgeon, who assured him that he was as sound as a bell, and that the woman had almost certainly never had the disease at all. Shelley, however, imagined that the surgeon was merely humouring him pityingly as one of the doomed. Nor did his fears stop short at himself: he would open the bosom of Hogg's shirt several times a day, and sigh bitterly over what he imagined he saw beneath. Hogg gives a racy description of the whole episode.[1] It was several weeks before Shelley was himself again. Enough has been already said to explain and justify to the full Hogg's statement:—
' He was altogether incapable of rendering an account of any transaction whatsoever according to the strict and precise truth, and the bare naked realities of actual life; not through an addiction to falsehood, which he cordially detested, but because he was the creature, the unsuspecting and unresisting victim, of his irresistible imagination.'

III

Further instances of 'semi-delusion', or what appears to be such, might be easily supplied; but we may now pass to another class of abnormality in Shelley's spiritual vision, and one which has a direct relation to certain elements in his poetry. From earliest childhood he had taken the liveliest interest in the supernatural. 'Sometimes', Hogg tells us, 'he watched the livelong nights for ghosts', and his researches into electricity and

[1] *Life of Shelley*, vol. i, chap. 10.

galvanism, which were to be resumed so ardently in his
.Oxford days, were varied by the eager perusal of
volumes on magic and witchcraft. With the help of the
rules herein presented, he even tried to raise a ghost
himself, uttering incantations and drinking thrice out of
a human skull (or its substitute) as he bestrode a running
stream. His sister Hellen testifies to his early love of
ghost stories, and of Monk Lewis's weirdly grotesque
poems. Later, *The Monk* itself, with all its wonders
and horrors, became one of his ' especial favourites ', and
Medwin tells us that he was also enraptured by ' a strange
wild romance entitled *Zofloya the Moor*, a Monk Lewisy
production where his Satanic Majesty, as in *Faust*, plays
the chief part '. He was also entranced by Bürger's
eery and gripping *Lenore*, by the witch Lorrinite in
Kehama, and by the legend of the headless. spectre of
St. Leonard's forest. This course of reading was at
once the cause and the effect of his fervent preoccupation
with the supernatural, and it affected his life no less
powerfully than it did his novels and his poetry.
Halliday's testimony to this effect has been already
quoted ; and of this period he tells us himself, in the
Hymn to Intellectual Beauty :

> While yet a boy I sought for ghosts, and sped
> Through many a listening chamber, cave, and ruin,
> And starlight wood, with fearful steps pursuing
> Hopes of high talk with the departed dead.
> I called on poisonous names with which our youth
> is fed.

Medwin tells us that at this period he was subject to
dreams of fearful vividness, to somnambulism, and to
waking visions. Hogg informs us that even at Oxford
Shelley had a ' decided inclination for magic, daemon-
ology, incantations, raising the dead, evoking spirits and

devils, seeing ghosts, and chatting familiarly with
apparitions.' While at Oxford, too, he read *Gebir*
eagerly, and we may well believe that he had a special
liking for that Book of it which tells how, at Masar,

Yet were remaining some of ancient race,
And ancient arts were now their sole delight.
With Time's first sickle they had marked the hour
When at their incantation would the Moon
Start back, and shuddering shed blue blasted light.

Several years later, in a letter of 1816, he speaks
sympathetically of the belief in ghosts, and condemns as
illogical the theory of Byron and 'Monk' Lewis that
none could entertain that belief without also believing in
God. Like Blake at this time he believed that the atmosphere surrounding the earth was peopled with the
spirits of the departed. Less frequently than Blake he
was vouchsafed, or conceived himself to have been vouchsafed, a vision of such beings. Shortly before his death
and after Allegra's, while walking by the moonlit ocean,
he claimed to have seen a naked child (Allegra) 'rise
from the sea and clap its hands as in joy, smiling at him'.[1]
A month later, while walking on the terrace of Villa
Magni after a succession of frightful dreams, he declared
that he had encountered his own wraith, which
addressed to him the boding question, 'How long do
you mean to be content?' The voice which he heard
at Rome calling on him to write *The Cenci* was probably
merely the casual utterance of a passing ragcrier, but the
fact that he construed it as supernatural, and at once
applied it to himself, illustrates at once the speed and
the unruliness of his imagination. His mind constantly
became the prey of his rebellious fancy: thus, after
repeating aloud the passage in *Christabel* describing the

[1] Williams, *Journal*, May 6, 1822.

gruesome mystery of Geraldine's bosom, he ran shrieking from the room, saying 'that he had suddenly thought of a woman he had heard of who had eyes instead of nipples; which taking hold of his mind horrified him'. This visionary faculty of Shelley's had its counterpart in his extraordinarily sensitive physical organization, and displayed itself vividly in his everyday demeanour. He tells us (Letter 274, December 7, 1817) that during a period of ill-health his feelings were 'awakened to a state of such unnatural and keen excitement that, only to instance the organ of sight, I find the very blades of grass and the boughs of distant trees present themselves to me with microscopical distinctness'. To beholders, during and after his visions he had the look of one possessed, and his eyes were filled with an unearthly light of heaven or of hell. It is curious to compare Medwin's description of him during these visitations with Hogg's: 'He was given to waking dreams', says Medwin, 'a sort of lethargy and abstraction that became habitual to him, and after the *accès* was over, his eyes flashed, his lips quivered, his voice was tremulous with emotion, a sort of ecstasy came over him, and he talked more like a spirit or an angel than a human being.' Hogg lays still greater stress on the daemonic aspect which Shelley sometimes assumed. 'Bysshe looked as he always looked, wild, intellectual, unearthly; like a spirit that had just descended from the sky; like a demon risen at that moment out of the ground'; and he adds, 'his poems seem to have been breathed, not by a mere mortal, but by some God or demon. His writings are invariably demoniacal, plainly the compositions of a demoniacal man.' It is curious that Shelley, in talking to Medwin, refers to himself as being occasionally daemoniacally possessed : ' The poet is a different being from the rest of the world.   Imagination steals over him —he knows not whence.   Images float before him—he knows not their home.   Struggling and contending powers are engendered within him, which no outward impulse, no inward passion awakened.   He utters sentiments he never meditated.   He creates persons whose original he had never seen.   But he cannot command the power that called them out of nothing.   He must wait till the God or daemon genius breathes it into him.'

We have already seen that Shelley, shortly before his death, believed he had had a visit from his own wraith. Jane Williams, according to Medwin, had seen the same apparition on a different occasion.   Byron tells us that ' some friends of Shelley, sitting together one evening, had seen him distinctly, as they thought, walk into a wood at Venice, when at the same moment, as they afterwards discovered, he was far away in quite a different direction.'   A fanciful mind might believe that this was Shelley's darker self walking apart from its celestial guardian.

In all these cases we find Shelley's mind working in strange and sometimes sinister fashion, through abnormal, or supernormal, correlation to the phenomenal world.   Out of his very yearning for the Absolute he had lost sure footing in the Particular.   Striving to soar into the empyrean before the day appointed to the human soul for flight, he fell repeatedly to earth, and, dazed by that shock, at times saw the things around him dizzily and brokenly.   Olympian at soul, he had not the Titan's gift of embracing mother earth and gaining strength and sanity thereby.   Like the cave-dwellers of his beloved Plato, when he returned to the cavern from the daylight, he saw the shadows on its walls less clearly than they were seen by his fellows of the lower vision who had never looked upon the sun. Had he dwelt longer in the world's cave perhaps his eyes would have grown clear and steady, would have focussed to the mean distances of earth, while abating nothing of their heavenly range and brightness. Certainly this steadier tendency seems to have been growing in him when his death at twenty-nine thwarted its full realization.

IV

As things were, his preoccupation with the ideal warped his views of men and women no less than his views of the external world, and frequently resulted in conduct not the less cruel and unjust to its victims because it was perfectly sincere on his part. In no matter is this tendency more marked than in his relations with women. It is unnecessary and impossible here to discuss in detail his relations with his first wife. In regard to this tragic matter, the most hotly canvassed incident of all Shelley's life, it is sufficient to say that he married Harriet Westbrook through chivalry rather than for love: that she was no fit mate for him in intellect or sympathy: that his desertion of her was first and fore-most due, not as has been occasionally pretended, to her coldness towards him, but to his infatuation for Mary Godwin. There is small reason for our believing what he pretended to believe, or quite possibly re~lly did believe, that she had been guilty of infidelity to him before he left her. If we are to credit Hogg, it would be unjust to ascribe to Shelley full responsibility for her suicide, since she was afflicted with suicidal mania long before he fled from her.[1] We may notice, however, in passing two matters, highly significant for good or evil, of the astonishing unworldliness displayed by Shelley in his relations with women : in the first place, he actually invited Harriet to join him and Mary in Switzerland after the elopement.[2] Secondly, being in need of funds, he begged and received money from Harriet after his flight with her rival.[3] Still more relevant to our purpose are his remarkable relations with Elizabeth Hitchener. He first met the schoolmistress of Hurstpierpoint in the summer of 1811, when he was nineteen and she twenty-nine. She was romantic and given to metaphysical speculation, and she found in Shelley a congenial comrade in her spiritual adventures. Though he only saw her twice again during the eighteen months which followed, they corresponded freely and exchanged impassioned views as to God, the soul and the hereafter. Immediately after his marriage with Harriet he wrote to Elizabeth, hailing her as 'the sister of his soul', and he subsequently invited her to stay with him and his wife at York and Keswick. Greatly to her honour, she had previously refused to share his property with his sisters and Hogg. The correspondence continued during Shelley's Irish trip, and when he returned to England he appealed passionately to Elizabeth to join Harriet and himself at Lynmouth and share their happiness. The invitation was seconded by Harriet herself, and eventually Elizabeth arrived, greatly to Shelley's delight. Subsequently she accompanied him and Harriet to Wales and London. At first she seems to have been

[1] Nor can we attribute responsibility to Shelley for the suicide of Fanny Godwin, Mary's half-sister, even if, as was maintained by Godwin and others, she took laudanum for love of him.

[2] Ingpen, Letter 194.   [3] Ingpen, Letter 197.

quite a success, for Harriet in a letter praises her industry and good spirits. There is no fair evidence that she was deceitful or disloyal to any one in the household, or that she had consciously concealed any side of her character from Shelley since the day when he first met her: yet within three months of her arrival he had grown utterly disgusted with her, and within four months, she was forced to leave his London household as though in disgrace. Doubtless his changed attitude toward her was in great part due to the representations of Harriet and her sister Eliza, and it is to Shelley's credit that after her departure he was prepared to pay her an annuity of £100 a year. But no money payment could possibly have compensated for her humiliation. The intensity of the reaction in Shelley's mind against his earlier idealization of her is painfully illustrated by the following passage of his letter (Ingpen, 158) to Hogg :—
'The Brown Demon, as we call our late tormentor and schoolmistress, must receive her stipend. I pay it with a heavy heart and an unwilling hand ; but it must be so. She was deprived by our misjudging haste of a situation where she was going smoothly: and now she says that her reputation is gone, her health ruined, her peace of mind destroyed by my barbarity ; a complete victim to all the woes, mental and bodily, that heroine ever suffered! This is not all fact ; but certainly she is embarrassed and poor, and we being in some degree the cause, we ought to obviate it. She is an artful, superficial, ugly, hermaphroditical beast of a woman, and my astonishment at my fatuity, inconsistency, and bad taste was never so great as after living four months with her as an inmate. What would Hell be were such a woman in Heaven ?'

This episode in Shelley's life has been described in full because it illustrates strikingly the aspect of his nature which immediately concerns us here. There were few of his women friends who did not suffer in greater or less degree through the disillusionment consequent on his early idealization of them. Thus, in 1812 he describes Eliza Westbrook as 'rather superior to the generality', and 'a very amiable girl': but two years later he says, 'I certainly hate her with all my heart and soul', and he calls her a 'blind and loathsome worm, that cannot see to sting'. Early in 1821 he had worshipped Emilia Viviani, for what then seemed to him her beauty and goodness; and in February of that year he wrote *Epipsychidion*, with its enraptured praise of her:—

> Seraph of Heaven! too gentle to be human,
> Veiling beneath that radiant form of Woman
> All that is insupportable in thee
> Of light and love and immortality!
> Sweet Benediction in the eternal Curse!
> Veiled Glory of this lampless Universe!

But in June of the same year he writes to John Gisborne: 'The *Epipsychidion* I cannot look at; the person whom it celebrates was a cloud instead of a Juno, and poor Ixion starts from the centaur that was the offspring of his own embrace.'

Even in his married life with Mary, and his ardent, if Platonic, friendships with Maria Gisborne and Jane Williams, clear traces of the same tendency are to be found.

I have already quoted Hogg's testimony as to the remarkable fascination which Shelley exercised over women, and the lively interest he inspired in every woman in the family the moment he entered the house.

Shelley himself has told us that in a previous incarnation he had loved Antigone, and that this made him find no content in any mortal tie. It will easily be seen that if this were his state of soul, there was a probability, even a certainty, of grave trouble. The remark of his which has just been quoted explains his whole relationship with women, and a great part of his attitude towards the world at large. His behaviour towards the opposite sex was occasioned by an idealism utterly out of keeping with the basic facts of human nature, and by the bitter and constant disillusionment in which such idealism must always result. Probably most of us have met in ordinary life people who have cast us out of their favour for the crime of being ourselves, and not the impossible and intolerable saint of their own dreams. The romantic side of such imagining is well illustrated in the love-story of Vigny and Dorval, the humorously sinister in Samuel Butler's great novel, *The Way of All Flesh*. It is easy to say that such imagining is merely the obverse of idealism : but probably this view of the matter did not commend itself at the time to the 'hermaphroditical beast of a woman' or the 'blind and loathsome worm'.

V

When we leave Shelley's life for his writings, the 'daemonic' element manifests itself under different forms. Among the most common of them is his constant preoccupation with putrefaction and decay. It is easy to dismiss this as a mere youthful foible of excess derived from his reading of *The Monk* and *Zofloya*; but unless he had already had that in him which responded eagerly to these wild volumes, he would never have read them so keenly nor have followed them so closely

as he did in his own romances, *Zastrozzi* and *St. Irvyne*.
The lighter aspect of this preoccupation is well
illustrated by the hoaxing warning which Shelley and
his sister Elizabeth sent to Edward Fergus Graham
(Ingpen, 4):—' Mind and keep yourself concealed, as my
Mother brings a blood-stained stiletto which she
purposes to make you bathe in the life-blood of her
enemy. Never mind the Death-demons and skeletons
dripping with the putrefaction of the grave which
occasionally may blast your straining eyeball.—
Persevere, even though Hell and destruction should
yawn beneath your feet.' The same preoccupation
recurs in the detailed descriptions furnished in *Zastrozzi*
and *St. Irvyne* respectively of the murder of Julia, and
the suicide of Olympia: and in such a passage as this,
describing the death by poison of Cavigni: 'Cavigni
quaffed the liquor to the dregs! The cup fell from his
trembling hand. The chill dew of death sat upon his
forehead: in terrific convulsions he fell headlong and,
inarticulately uttering " I am poisoned ", sank seemingly
lifeless on the earth. . . . Wolfstein advanced to the
body, unappalled by the crime he had committed; and
tore aside the vest from its bosom; that bosom was dis-
coloured by large spots of livid purple, which, by their
premature appearance, declared the poison which had
been used to destroy him to be excessively powerful.'

It may be convenient here to discuss briefly the sinister elements of these two portentous works so as to
avoid the ordeal of returning to them. Outside
gruesome dreams, neither novel deals greatly in the
supernatural variety of the sinister which occurs elsewhere in Shelley. Both thus differ considerably from
their prototype *The Monk*. The initiation of Ginotti

and the death of Wolfstein in *St. Irvyne* do, it is true,
partake of the crudely miraculous : but apart from the
horrors and surprises scattered throughout the pages,
the most sinister element in each novel, and especially
in *Zastrozzi*, is its master-motive of revenge. These
stories must, of course, be regarded for the most part
as mere exercises of boyish fancy : but their pages,
spattered with blood and hate, are in striking contrast to
the lesson so emphatically preached a year later by
Shelley in *The Address to the Irish People*, that revolu-
tionists can under no circumstance be justified in assert-
ing their national rights by bloodshed. As a matter
of fact, we know from Hogg that Shelley hated the
idea of taking life in any form. Yet constantly throughout his earlier poems does one encounter the reek of the
slaughter-yard and whiff of the charnel-vault. In his
fragmentary poem of 1807, the night-raven sings tidings
of approaching death. In *A Dialogue* (1809) Death
appears indeed as the consoler, and love is exempted
from his touch : and in *To Death*, the mortal triumphs
over his dissolution. But when we come to the *Poems
of Victor and Cazire*, and other of Shelley's juvenile
poems (1810), we find *St. Edmond's Eve* to be a crude
study in the terrible, and *Revenge* and *Ghasta* to be
mere metrical novelettes of sensation written in the vein
of *Zastrozzi*. The scene, crude and unreal as some
melodrama staged in a child's theatre, is lit, as it were,
from the wings, with stage lightnings, blue firelight, and
the ' midnight pestiferous meteor's blaze '—illuminations
afterwards to be flung with quite other effect on
Shelley's later work. And beneath this rococo heaven
stalk daemons, nightmares, tombless ghosts, and even
the skeleton of a dead man, its half-eaten eyeballs

illuminated by two pale flames. Fiends laugh and howl over the corpse of a man who has sold his soul to hell. Other corpses rot and stink around, and 'the loathsome worm' gnaws below in 'the dark mansions of the dead'. Nor in *Queen Mab*, for all its promise, and occasional achievement, of beauty, are we ever far from that 'gloomy power whose reign is in the tainted sepulchres'. Putrefaction persists everywhere, even if it does not utterly prevail. Even when Nature is invoked in her own fair shrine we are forbidden to forget the worm 'that lurks in graves and fattens on the dead'. In every corner pestilence 'lowers expectant'.[1] Human flesh poisons the atmosphere with putrid smoke,[2] and over the whole scene there is moonlight, not soft and gracious as at the close of *The Merchant of Venice*, but weird and lurid as in that great poem of Landor's in which Shelley had just been steeping his keenly responsive imagination. Among Shelley's later poems there is scarcely one of any length which is totally free from the atmosphere of corruption. Especially common are the references to the 'charnel' and the 'worm'. Early in *The Revolt of Islam* we meet 'Death, Decay, Earthquake and Blight and Want and Madness pale, wingèd and wan diseases'. Later, when Pestilence meets Laon, she prints on his lips 'the Plague's blue kisses'. Later still she lays a mocking feast of bread, and sets around it 'a ring of cold, stiff babes'. Again, we inhale the 'rotting vapour' that passes from the unburied dead, and are told that when the beasts' food fails, they inhale 'the breath of its

[1] Cf. *Falsehood and Vice*, quoted in the note on IV. 178-9 of *Queen Mab*.

[2] Cf. the reference to religion in *Falsehood and Vice*:

The dreadful stench of her torches' flare
Fed with human fat polluted the air.

decay', while a strange disease glows in their green eyes: the sea-shore stinks with dead and putrid fish: human flesh is sold for food in the market place: blue Plague falls upon the race of man, and near the great fountain in the public square, a pyramid of corpses crumbles beneath the noonday sun. The zest with which Shelley's imagination works on this subject may be gauged from such a stanza as the following:

It was not hunger now, but thirst. Each well
    Was choked with rotting corpses, and became
A cauldron of green mist made visible
    At sunrise. Thither still the myriads came,
    Seeking to quench the agony of the flame,
Which raged like poison through their bursting
        veins;
    Naked they were from torture, without shame,
Spotted with nameless scars and lurid blains,
Childhood, and youth, and age, writhing in savage
        pains.

The union of passion with decay developed with such sinister mastery in Swinburne's *The Leper* appears in these lines:

A woman's shape, now lank and cold and blue,
    The dwelling of the many-coloured worm,
Hung there; the white and hollow cheek I drew
    To my dry lips—what radiance did inform
    Those horny eyes? whose was that withered form?
Alas, alas! it seemed that Cythna's ghost
    Laughed in those looks, and that the flesh was warm
Within my teeth!—A whirlwind keen as frost
Then in its sinking gulfs my sickening spirit tossed.

It is re-echoed in Fiordispina's longing to lie beside her dead love in her shroud:

'And if my love were dead,
    Unless my heart deceives me, I would lie
Beside him in my shroud as willingly
    As now in the gay night-dress Lilla wrought.'

A similar touch occurs under symbolic form in the
Invocation to Misery :

> Hasten to the bridal bed—
> Underneath the grave 'tis spread :
> In darkness may our love be hid,
> Oblivion be our coverlid—
> We may rest, and none forbid.

In *Rosalind and Helen* we again come upon the dead in
their 'putrid shrouds', and upon the couplet :

> When she was a thing that did not stir
> And the crawling worms were cradling her :

in *Prometheus* the victims of the Fury are 'linked to
corpses in unwholesome cells'. But perhaps no better
instance could be given of Shelley's preoccupation with
putrefaction than *The Sensitive Plant*. As soon as the
lady dies, we are prepared for the horrors to follow by
being told that the Plant felt

> the smell, cold, oppressive, and dank,
> Sent through the pores of the coffin-plank.

As the garden becomes

> cold and foul
> Like the corpse of her who had been its soul,

the lilies grow

> drooping, and white, and wan,
> Like the head and the skin of a dying man.

A still more sinister passage appeared in the edition of
1820 but was subsequently cancelled :

> Their moss rotted off them, flake by flake,
> Till the thick stalk stuck like a murderer's stake,
> Where rags of loose flesh yet tremble on high,
> Infecting the winds that wander by.

In a later poem Shelley refers thus to the dead Ginevra :

> If it be death, when there is felt around
> A smell of clay, a pale and icy glare,

And silence, and a sense that lifts the hair
From the scalp to the ankles, as it were
Corruption from the spirit passing forth,
And giving all it shrouded to the earth,
And leaving as swift lightning in its flight
Ashes, and smoke, and darkness.

A few months before his death he thus commences
a song :

The rude wind is singing
The dirge of the music dead ;
The cold worms are clinging
Where kisses were lately fed.

The above cases are mainly ones of direct description :
even more significant of Shelley's preoccupation with
decay and the sinister are the similes which he constantly introduces in contexts where they are not
strictly necessary :

Two days thus passed—I neither raved nor died—
Thirst raged within me, like a scorpion's nest
Built in mine entrails.

These things dwelt in me, even as shadows keep
Their watch in some dim charnel's loneliness,
A shoreless sea, a sky sunless and planetless !

The twilight's gloom
Lay like a charnel's mist within the radiant dome.

The hope of torturing him smells like a heap
Of corpses, to a death-bird after battle.

And one sweet laugh, most horrible to hear,
As of a joyous infant waked and playing
With its dead mother's breast.

As from an ancestral oak
Two empty ravens sound their clarion,
Yell by yell, and croak by croak,
When they scent the noonday smoke
Of fresh human carrion.

From the cities where from caves,
Like the dead from putrid graves,
Troops of starvelings gliding come,
Living tenants of a tomb.

The heavy dead hulk
On the living sea rolls an inanimate bulk,
Like a corpse on the clay which is hungering to fold
Its corruption around it.

They stand aloof,
And are withdrawn—so that the world is bare;
As if a spectre wrapped in shapeless terror
Amid a company of ladies fair

Should glide and glow, till it became a mirror
Of all their beauty.

As dogs bay the moonlight clouds,
Which, like spectres wrapped in shrouds,
Pass o'er night in multitudes.

Of a type with these images is the sinister power which
Shelley imparts to Beatrice Cenci's imagining:

The sunshine on the floor is black! the air
Is changed to vapours such as the dead breathe
In charnel pits! Pah! I am choked! There creeps
A clinging, black, contaminating mist
About me . . . 'tis substantial, heavy, thick,
I cannot pluck it from me, for it glues
My fingers and my limbs to one another,
And eats into my sinews, and dissolves
My flesh to a pollution, poisoning
The subtle, pure, and inmost spirit of life!
My God! I never knew what the mad felt
Before; for I am mad beyond all doubt!
No, I am dead! These putrefying limbs
Shut round and sepulchre the panting soul
Which would burst forth into the wandering air!

In view of the foregoing considerations it is not too
much to claim that Shelley ranks with Baudelaire and
Poe as one of the poets of decay. His preoccupation
with the charnel and the worm, as exemplified in the

passages quoted above, suggest affinities with *The Conqueror Worm*, or the conclusion of *Annabel Lee*, or that strange story in which the corpse of M. Valdemar, when unmesmerized, rots suddenly away and lies on the bed ' a nearly liquid mass of loathsome, of detestable, putridity'. A similar, though not identical, quality appears in Baudelaire's poem, *Une Charogne*, in which a lover, walking with his beloved, espies a piece of decaying carrion, and moralizes thereon concerning his passion.[1]

Apart from descriptions of decay, Shelley's imagination has a strange power both of word and idea over the sinister in nature. There is a grim strength, for instance, in this recurring image of the scorpion wreaking venomed death upon itself under torture [2]:

> The truths of their pure lips, that never die,
> Shall bind the scorpion falsehood with a wreath
> Of ever-living flame,
> Until the monster sting itself to death.

> Each girt by the hot atmosphere
> Of his blind agony like a scorpion stung
> By his own rage upon his burning bier
> Of circling coals of fire.

There is a kindred variety of the sinister in such lines as:

> The slow soft toads out of damp corners creep,

and

> foodless toads
> Within voluptuous chambers panting crawled.

---

[1] There is much of this preoccupation with decay in modern French literature. Cf. Aloysius Bertrand, *Le Cheval Mort*, and *Claire de Lune*; Tristan Corbière, *Les Amours Jaunes* (e. g. the conclusion of *Le Bossu Bitord*).

[2] For other instances of this image, see the essay in this volume on *Shelley's Symbolism*.

Such are the more striking instances of what is perhaps the most conspicuous form of the sinister in Shelley's poetry.   It is quite impossible to dismiss this as either a youthful foible or a melodramatic trick of literary practice.   It corresponds to something deep and lasting in Shelley's soul.   It seems to be partly the result of a violent reaction against his ecstatic optimism and belief in the ultimate perfectibility of all nature, human and cosmic.   Beaten at certain crises from this hope, his mind fled desperately into the extreme of horror.   Seen in this aspect, the sinister in his verse has strong analogy with the sinister in his character, especially as manifested in his relations with women. In actual life his vagaries of this kind were, according to his own account, due to his having 'loved Antigone', and when we pass to the ideal universe we find him speaking of himself as desiring more in this world 'than any understand'.   Stripped of the ideal and its armour, his soul was laid bare to the torments of reality, and became the nerve 'o'er which do creep the else unfelt oppressions of this earth'.   The ecstatic physical intensity both of his yearning and of the subsequent reaction, is well illustrated in *To Constantia Singing*:

> Her voice is hovering o'er my soul—it lingers
>   O'ershadowing it with soft and lulling wings,
> The blood and life within those snowy fingers
>   Teach witchcraft to the instrumental strings.
> My brain is wild, my breath comes quick—
>   The blood is listening in my frame,
> And thronging shadows, fast and thick,
>   Fall on my overflowing eyes;
> My heart is quivering like a flame;
>   As morning dew, that in the sunbeam dies,
>   I am dissolved in these consuming ecstasies.

There is the same intensity in the fragmentary *Igniculus Desiderii*:

To thirst and find no fill—to wail and wander
With short unsteady steps—to pause and ponder—
To feel the blood run through the veins and tingle
Where busy thought and blind sensation mingle;
To nurse the image of unfelt caresses
Till dim imagination just possesses
The half-created shadow, then all the night
Sick. . . .

If one reads this poem carefully and compares with it Shelley's own account of the extraordinary acuteness which his senses developed during states of sickness, one can easily understand how inevitable it became that he who had seen and felt the beautiful with such abnormal vividness, should, when flung back on the terrible and horrible, feel and portray them also with appalling vividness in their minutest particulars. Equally applicable to his poetic vision and the hallucinations of his everyday life, is his description of 'that state of mind in which ideas may be supposed to assume the force of sensations through the confusion of thought with the objects of thought, and the excess of passion animating the creatures of imagination '.[1]

The last phase of Shelley's relationship with Emilia Viviani, a phase which might be called the sordid prose sequel of the exquisite *Epipsychidion*, is less the tragedy of Emilia herself than of Shelley's own genius and soul. In poetry as in life, his Antigone was constantly proving a mere Emilia, or even an Elizabeth Hitchener, to be at once twisted in the glass of his imagining into the semblance of a 'brown demon'. Yet salvation came to him from the very cause of these women's

---

[1] Note to *Hellas*.

discomfiture : for as each of their dwindled shapes passed rejected from his life, so surely did he recapture in Antigone his ideal of truth and loveliness, only to desert that certainty once more for the lying and fleeting forms of flesh and blood.

VI

Closely akin to this is another striking characteristic of Shelley's thought and verse. On the one hand he believed with all his heart that evil is not the primary but the secondary principle of life, that the human soul is in its nature good, and only needs awakening to understand and realize a golden perfection of charity and brotherhood ; and that the basic principle of all existence, human and cosmic, is love. This belief is the central tenet of his faith : it inspires many of his most perfect lyrics, and is the soul of *The Revolt of Islam*, *Prometheus Unbound*, and *Hellas*. Yet side by side with this strain in Shelley, a totally different one sounds throughout his poetry, and constitutes him one of the great poets of despair. The self-portrayal which had begun in *Alastor* deepens in *Prince Athanase* into a settled gloom of heart and brain. It has never been doubted that in this poem Shelley is attempting a portrait of himself, part dream, part reality. Here we are told that he is consumed by a grief unmirrored in other minds, by 'thoughts on thoughts, unresting multitudes', which worked within him 'as the fiends which wake and feed an everliving woe'. At the end of the First Part of this poem, Shelley relinquished as morbid [1] his description of Athanase, after having written the following lines :

[1] See his Note to this passage.

> like an eyeless nightmare grief did sit
> Upon his being; a snake which fold by fold
> Pressed out the life of life, a clinging fiend
> Which clenched him if he stirred with deadlier hold ;
> And so his grief remained—let it remain—untold!

He touches the inmost secret of his own character, in all
its inconsistency and aspiration and disillusion, when he
says of the Prince

> all who knew and loved him then perceived
> That there was drawn an adamantine veil
>
> Between his heart and mind,—both unrelieved
> Wrought in his brain and bosom separate strife.

It would seem that with Shelley himself, heart and brain,
taken separately, were true and strong! the pity was
that in the fight against circumstance they so seldom
joined forces, and were thus so often vanquished and led
captive by disillusion and despair.   Hence the mood and
the music we find in *Mutability*, the song, *Rarely, rarely,
comest thou, Spirit of Delight*, and *Lines Written in
Dejection near Naples* :

> Yet now despair itself is mild,
>   Even as the winds and waters are ;
> I could lie down like a tired child,
>   And weep away the life of care
>   Which I have borne and yet must bear,
> Till death like sleep might steal on me,
>   And I might feel in the warm air
> My cheek grow cold, and hear the sea
> Breathe o'er my dying brain its last monotony.

Hence, too, the famous portrait he draws of himself
in *Adonais* as 'a herd-abandoned deer struck by the
hunter's dart', and as

> A pardlike Spirit beautiful and swift—
> A love in desolation masked ;—a Power
> Girt round with weakness ;—it can scarce uplift
> The weight of the superincumbent hour ;

T

It is a dying lamp, a falling shower,
A breaking billow;—even whilst we speak
Is it not broken? On the withering flower
The killing sun smiles brightly : on a cheek
The life can burn in blood, even while the heart
    may break.

Hence, again, we find him in *The False Laurel and the True*, answering an imaginary interlocutor thus :

Ah, friend, 'tis the false laurel that I wear;
Bright though it seem, it is not the same
    As that which bound Milton's immortal hair;
Its dew is poison; and the hopes that quicken
    Under its chilling shade, though seeming fair,
Are flowers which die almost before they sicken.[1]

VII

In the passages quoted above from *Queen Mab* and *The Sensitive Plant*, Shelley evidently scorns beauty of subject, and strives to portray the sinister for its own sake, trusting his own imagination to envelop it with daemonic glamour : a more positive and acceptable phase of the same instinct is his constant attempt to discover beauty in things generally considered sinister. This effort is evident in the original theme of the relationship between the lovers in *The Revolt of Islam*, in Shelley's development of a kindred motive in *The Cenci*, and in his famous remark that this motive is 'a very poetical circumstance'. It appears again in his portrayal of the Spirit of Good as a snake in *The Revolt of Islam*, in his making the Woman take it to her bosom and scornfully repudiate any fear of it, and in the eventual absorption of its serpentine beauty in the transfigured glory of Laon :

[1] Cf. *Lines written in the Bay of Lerici*, 27—end.

Then first, two glittering lights were seen to glide
    In circles on the amethystine floor,
Small serpent eyes trailing from side to side,
    Like meteors on a river's grassy shore,
    They round each other rolled, dilating more
And more—then rose, commingling into one,
    One clear and mighty planet hanging o'er
A cloud of deepest shadow, which was thrown
Athwart the glowing steps and the crystalline throne.

Again, in *Rosalind and Helen* the pale snake floats on the
' dark and lucid flood in the light of his own loveliness '.
In *Adonais* 'the green lizard and the golden snake like
unimprisoned flames out of their trance awake'.[1] And
again, in *Prometheus Unbound*, after the transfiguration
occurring in the Third Act, toads, snakes, and efts
become at once beautiful ' with little change of shape
or hue.'

The simile of the meteors in the lines just quoted from
The Revolt of Islam is itself a good case in point. The
meteor, a thing of fear or evil with most poets, is constantly in Shelley beautiful and benignant.[2] Here it is
used as a symbol of the snake, which is frequently itself
the symbol of Shelley's antinomianism, and of his conviction that the highest good is often what the world
holds to be most evil. He was as great a transvaluer
of values as Nietzsche, and this in art not less than in
life. It is noteworthy that the rare beauty of Laon's
hall is compounded of
            Starry shapes between
And horned moons and meteors strange and fair.

Yet another benignant meteor, speeding from its home

---

[1] Compare the fragmentary ' Wake the serpent not ', &c.

[2] Shelley's use of the symbol of the meteor is more fully described
in another essay in this volume. Here, a few examples only are
given for the sake of illustration.

of decay, appears later in the poem to light the reunited pair in their love, and reappears under a form of strange beauty in *Marenghi*:

> And the marsh-meteors, like tame beasts, at night
>   Came licking with blue tongues his veinèd feet;
> And he would watch them, as, like spirits bright,
>   In many entangled figures quaint and sweet
> To some enchanted music they would dance—
> Until they vanished at the first moon-glance.

'The tempestuous loveliness of terror' is hymned with a different reference in the lines on the Medusa of Leonardo da Vinci, 'whose horror and whose beauty are divine':

> Yet it is less the horror than the grace
>   Which turns the gazer's spirit into stone,
> Whereon the lineaments of that dead face
>   Are graven, till the characters be grown
> Into itself, and thought no more can trace;
> 'Tis the melodious hue of beauty thrown
> Athwart the darkness and the glare of pain,
> Which humanize and harmonize the strain.

Akin to this is the homage Shelley pays[1] to the Hermaphrodite, that 'sweet marble monster of both sexes', dear also to Gautier and Swinburne.

A main characteristic of his genius, and one closely akin to the foregoing, and definitely connected with his use of the sinister, is his desire to restore their full dues to objects whose beauty has been undervalued: thus in *The Witch of Atlas* he says:

> Men scarcely know how beautiful fire is—
>   Each flame of it is as a precious stone
> Dissolved in ever-moving light, and this
>   Belongs to each and all who gaze upon.

---

[1] Fragment connected with *Epipsychidion*, ll. 60-1.

And in the same way he tells how Prometheus

> tamed fire, which, like some beast of prey,
> Most terrible, but lovely, played beneath
> The frown of man.

Here it is once more the combination of loveliness and terror which fascinates him, as it had previously fascinated Collins.

Some of Shelley's most beautiful poetry of Nature possesses a peculiar unearthliness which seems due to a desire to get as far away as possible from the normal and everyday aspects of her which were so dear to Wordsworth. A good example of this is the picture of the sea-bed and its flowers given in the *Ode to the West Wind*:

> Thou
> For whose path the Atlantic's level powers
>
> Cleave themselves into chasms, while far below
> The sea-blooms and the oozy woods which wear
> The sapless foliage of the ocean, know
>
> Thy voice, and suddenly grow grey with fear,
> And tremble and despoil themselves: oh, hear!

A like magic appears in *Prometheus Unbound*, in the Second Faun's description of the spirit's home:

> I have heard those more skilled in spirits say,
> The bubbles, which the enchantment of the sun
> Sucks from the pale faint water-flowers that pave
> The oozy bottom of clear lakes and pools,
> Are the pavilions where such dwell and float
> Under the green and golden atmosphere
> Which noontide kindles through the woven leaves;
> And when these burst, and the thin fiery air,
> The which they breathed within those lucent domes,
> Ascends to flow like meteors through the night,
> They ride on them, and rein their headlong speed,
> And bow their burning crests, and glide in fire
> Under the waters of the earth again.

Nor does this unearthliness depend merely on Shelley's choice of subject: it recurs constantly in the colour given by his imagination even to the normal features of Nature.   Nobody but he would have conceived this image for the Moon:

> And like a dying lady, lean and pale,
> Who totters forth, wrapped in a gauzy veil,
> Out of her chamber, led by the insane
> And feeble wanderings of her fading brain,
> The moon arose up in the murky East,
> A white and shapeless mass.

This unearthly colouring is sometimes extended even to Nature's homeliest aspects: witness the strange beauty given to the simplest flowers in *The Question*—beauty due in large measure to the hues of night cast upon the spring daylight by the 'moonlight-coloured may', and by the water lilies

> Which lit the oak that overhung the hedge
> With moonlight beams of their own watery light.

Starting from the merely horrible and sinister, we have arrived almost insensibly at one of the most real and distinctive kinds of beauty in all Shelley's verse. It would be as easy as it is unnecessary to follow the chain on to its final link, and show how that beauty passes into the simpler, more usual and normal, and perhaps also more perfect, beauty of *Life of Life*, or *The Hymn of Apollo*, or *Love's Philosophy*.   It would be easy, too, to enlarge further on the psychological aspect of the matter, and to continue the parallel between Shelley's poetry and his life.   In each he had a vision of glory withheld from his fellows, and, when this was eclipsed, he at times moved dizzily amid a night of tombs and terrors.   In the darker places of his soul's adventure amid poetry, he was haunted by spectres of his own imagining, even as in life he had been haunted by his phantom assailant of the Pisa post-office, and the visionary assassin of Tanyrallt. And even when he came forth into the daylight and caught and sang its beauty, his song had constantly something in it of the night's witchery and terror. 'The oracular vapour' he had 'drunk wandering in his youth' would at times turn to other things than 'truth, virtue, love or joy'. Of the two powers to which he had ascribed poetic inspiration, God or the daemon genius, it was often the daemon that held him, or in his own words,

> This fiend whose ghastly presence ever
> Beside thee like thy shadow hangs.

The condition described in this and similar passages was, one must repeat, a deadly reality with Shelley, and is on no account to be dismissed as a mere literary affectation or extravagance : on the other hand, we must never forget that if there was something of the sinister deep in his soul and song, this was but the obverse of that celestial effluence hardly touched on here—the effluence of Love, whom he

> sent to bind
> The disunited tendrils of that vine
> Which bears the wine of life, the human heart,

the effluence of Beauty through which his hearers walk

> exempt from mortal care
> Godlike, o'er the clear billows of sweet sound.

NATURE IN WORDSWORTH AND MEREDITH

THE first duty incumbent on any one who attempts to discuss Nature is to say what he means by this terribly misleading word, the uses and ambiguities of which are numerous, and as old as the history of thought itself. For our present purpose it is chiefly important to distinguish between two of these. In one sense Nature has been taken to mean the whole universe, including God, the cosmos and its creatures, the mind of man, and all that is, or may be imagined. In this sense, every poet and thinker is consciously or unconsciously an interpreter of Nature, and every being and thing a symbol of her. It is this Nature that Arnold has in mind when he makes Empedocles say:

> All things the world which fill
> Of but one stuff are spun,
> That we who rail are still,
> With what we rail at, one;
> One with the o'er-laboured Power that through the breadth and length
>
> Of earth and air and sea,
> In men and plants and stones,
> Hath toil perpetually,
> And travails, pants, and moans;
> Fain would do all things well, but sometimes fails in strength.

The other sense of the word—in modern times, certainly the more common one—denotes the power

external to human-kind which informs earth and sky
and sea and all that is in them save only man; the
power which evolution has shown to be man's mother,
but between which and him there is fixed a great gulf of
conscience and reason—the power whom men have
alternately execrated as man's cruellest enemy, and
worshipped as his kindly mistress or benign saint. It
is chiefly in this latter sense that the word Nature will
be used in the present essay, though one incursion
or more will be made into the wider realm.

If we take Nature in this sense, it is clear that in reading Wordsworth and Meredith, the two among modern
English poets who have seen most deeply into her
meaning, we find essential resemblances and essential
differences. Our present attempt will be to deal successively with both of these, and then to inquire how
far the intuition of Nature expressed by each poet
satisfies the consciousness and imagination of ordinary
men and women. And, first, for the resemblances
between the two.

It is obvious, at the outset, that each brought to his
study and interpretation of Nature certain supreme
qualities—those of close and loving observation, deep
understanding and sympathy, and profound and luminous
imagination. It is also obvious that in the determination
which their genius gave to these qualities, they resemble
one another, and differ in essentials from all but a very
few of their predecessors. Imaginative delight in
Nature was, indeed, no new thing in the history of
poetry; it appears in forms of perfect beauty in the
choruses of Sophocles, in the *Georgics* of Virgil, and in
the Sonnets of Shakespeare. For sheer sensuous
delight in natural beauty, for the play of exquisite fancy

upon wood and stream and hill, not Wordsworth himself
has rivalled certain of the Elizabethans—Shakespeare,
for instance, and Spenser. Nor, of course, is this
delight *merely* sensuous ; Nature is frequently, especially
in Shakespeare, made the symbol and the mirror of the
varying moods of man's thought and feeling; and
though shortly after Shakespeare's age the fire burnt
low for nearly a century and a half, it flamed forth once
more in some of Wordsworth's immediate forerunners
—in Chatterton, and Burns, and Blake—and burnt with
a quieter glow in the poetry of Thomson and Cowper.
Nor would any account of the modern interpretation of
Nature, whether in prose or in poetry, in England or
elsewhere, be complete without mention of the great
name of Rousseau. It would be ridiculous, then, to
contend that imagination of a high order was first
applied to Nature by Wordsworth or his immediate
predecessors. It is certain, on the other hand, that
during Wordsworth's age, both in England and on the
Continent, the imaginative interpretation of Nature
differed rather in kind than in degree from that of
previous ages. As far as English poetry is concerned,
though such interpretation had been implicit in certain
of Wordsworth's forerunners, it first achieved full consciousness in him, it led him deeper into the heart of
things than they had ever gone, and became the basis,
not only of some of the greatest of modern poetry, but
of a transcendent faith and philosophy of life. Of this
faith or philosophy, embodying as it does the conception
of Nature as Healer and Revealer, more will be said in
the latter half of this essay.

This deepening of imaginative consciousness depends
closely on a second main quality, which differentiates

our two poets, in their attitude towards Nature, from all but a few of their immediate predecessors. This was the quality, so closely akin to imagination, of close and loving observation.[1] With many previous poets this had been superseded by fancy, lit, indeed, by constant gleams of Nature's splendour, but not consciously seeking her fuller revelation, and content to follow its own lure-light wherever that might lead. These had sought rather to enjoy Nature's passing favours than to woo her passionately, and to win her soul. Their mighty imagination had not yet been given wholly to her service and love. To many of the Elizabethans, Nature had been but as a beautiful woman, the captive of their bow and spear, whom they decked out bravely in the splendour of their fancy, whose beauty graced their joys, and in some wise calmed their sorrows, and whom at times they sought to bring in, Vashti-like, that she might heighten the bright feast of life at which they sat. Thus, to Drayton, the flowers are 'brave embroidered girls', the blossoming trees show 'like gorgeous hangings on the walls of some rich, princely room', while Spenser sings of the lily:

> Lo, lo, how brave she decks her bounteous bower
>   With silken curtains and gold coverlets,
> Therein to shroud her sumptuous bellamoure!

[1] Professor Elton, in his *Survey of English Literature*, 1780–1830, writes :—'Wordsworth is one of the poets, like Milton, Pope, and Shelley, who has made, recorded, and kept a definite vow : he says that he was not more than fourteen when he first became aware " of the infinite variety of natural appearances which had been unnoticed by the poets of any age or country, so far as I was acquainted with them ; and I made a resolution to supply, in some degree, the deficiency." ' The quotation is from Wordsworth's note on *An Evening Walk*.

One character of Fletcher's speaks of

> The mighty Persian's daughter,
> Bright as the breaking East, as midday glorious,

and another says of his mistress:

> The orient morning breaking out in odours
> Is not so full of perfumes as her breath is.

And it is still the same note which rings in this deeper music of Middleton's (I have purposely omitted quotations from Shakespeare, as I wish to instance the type rather than the exception):—

> Upon whose lips, the sweet fresh buds of youth,
> The holy dew of prayer lies, like pearl
> Dropped from the opening eyelids of the morn
> Upon a bashful rose.

Nature had no lack of homage from the Elizabethans; but this sprang rather from passionate and exultant joy clothing itself in great poetry than from the conscious and profound reverence which is the soul of Wordsworth's inspiration. To Wordsworth, Nature was the mystical Mother, brooding on wondrous secrets, whose face her children must be ever watching with intensest scrutiny, and whose every word and gesture were fraught with mighty import. It was not enough to take her manifestations at haphazard, and transmute them wantonly into forms of one's own fancy. Man must interpret rather than embroider; and this he could only do through constant and loving vigil. Hence, with Wordsworth, as with Meredith, observation was set to work with a thoroughness till then unknown; and in both these poets it ranges from sheer sensuous delight in Nature's beauty to that profound mysticism which sees all earth and heaven in a single flower.

The first quality—that of sensuous delight in Nature—
is constantly evident in Wordsworth's poetry, though it
is seldom without some admixture of more profound
and conscious thought, here differing again from the
delight of the typical Elizabethan. In respect of his joy
in Nature, Wordsworth may, perhaps, be described as
a universalist. Byron is pre-eminently the poet of the
mountains, Swinburne the singer of the sea. Meredith
knew to the full the joy of the everlasting hills,[1] and has
limned certain moods of sky and stream more exquisitely
than perhaps any man yet; but, in his poetry, he is con-
spicuously the singer of the forest and its trees and
flowers and creatures; and Nature's symbol is with him
the Woods of Westermain. But Wordsworth's mind
played delightedly over every form of natural beauty,
were it hidden in the tiny shrine of the daisy or the
small celandine, or received with the shifting cloud-wrack
into the steady bosom of the lake, were it passionate
with 'the tumult of a tropic sky', utterly peaceful in the
Dell of Applethwaite or the pine-grove of Townend, or
pinnacled in solemn majesty on the brow of Black Comb
or Helvellyn, or 'among Skiddaw'. Others might
specialize; for Wordsworth's sympathy and love nothing
in Nature was too great or too little. It was, however,
in her simple and common, sometimes even in her
harsher and more austere aspects, that she appealed to
him most strongly. From early boyhood he had known

> the first virgin passion of a soul
> Communing with the glorious universe:[2]

His soul lacked not 'Aeolian visitations': he had felt

---

[1] Cf. *Beauchamp's Career*, chap ix; *The Amazing Marriage*,
beginning, &c., &c.

[2] *Excursion*, i. 285-6.

'gleams like the flashing of a shield': while still a boy,
as he rowed by stealth on Esthwaite in a borrowed boat,[1]
the mountain that towered above the lake had seemed
to make after him, 'as if with voluntary power instinct',
had overtaken him, and had carried the meaning of
Nature deep into his heart, so that for many days his
brain

> Worked with a dim and undetermined sense
> Of unknown modes of being.

Similarly, it was Nature who first brought home to the
rambling schoolboy the majesty of man. The sight of a
Cumbrian shepherd[2] seen as a giant through the mist
on the mountain side, or glorified by the deep radiance
of the setting sun, had ennobled man outwardly before
his sight, and brought him, mystically but surely, to an
unconscious love and reverence of human nature.

It was, indeed, already in boyhood that he learnt to feel
a deep association between natural manifestations and
the deeper moods of the human consciousness, and laid
up a host of memories which were afterwards to flash
upon his mind with inner meaning. This tendency is
evident in the beautiful passage in the *Prelude*[3] in
which he sees more deeply into both Nature and himself
as he associates the grief caused by his father's death with
the tempestuous point of vantage on the mountain side,
from which, a few days before the blow, he had been
watching for the ponies that were to take him home.
After this, he tells us :

> the wind and sleety rain,
> And all the business of the elements,
> The single sheep, and the one blasted tree,

---

[1] *Prelude*, i. 372–400.   [2] *Ibid.*, viii. 255-93.
[3] *Ibid.*, xii. 287-335.

And the bleak music from that old stone wall,
The noise of wood and water, and the mist
That on the line of each of those two roads
Advanced in such indisputable shapes—
All these were kindred spectacles and sounds
To which I oft repaired, and thence would drink
As at a fountain.

It will be seen from this passage, that Nature could
furnish Wordsworth not only with holiday garlands, but
with

sober posies of funereal flowers,
Gathered among those solitudes sublime
From formal gardens of the lady Sorrow:[1]

and could abide with him in such wise that even when
the first keen joy of youth had passed he could still say:

yet for me
Life's morning radiance hath not left the hills;
Her dew is on the flowers.[2]

The passage just quoted from the *Prelude* illustrates
well that faculty of observation which is common
to Wordsworth and Meredith, and differentiates them
from their predecessors.   Both of them might have said,
with Blake, 'Every minute particular is holy.'   Though
Wordsworth himself hotly repudiates the idea that
observation of Nature means taking a mere mechanical
inventory of her details, yet this reverent watching
of her is the very essence of his, as of Meredith's,
inspiration.   In one passage he tells us how, as he
looked intently on the lake:

the calm
And dead still water lay upon my mind,
Even with a weight of pleasure, and the sky,
Never before so beautiful, sank down
Into my heart and held me like a dream![3]

[1] *Prelude*, vi. 553-55.   [2] *Ibid.*, vi. 50-2.
[3] *Ibid.*, ii. 170-4.

This scrutiny, with its mystical culmination, had, of course, a far more profound effect than the creation of beautiful moods or beautiful lines of poetry. The 'wise passiveness' with which Wordsworth taught that Nature should be watched is no mere state of listless lethargy, but is the mystical consummation of the intense activity with which he taught she should be wooed. It is this intuition of her which produces the essential beauty of more than one of the Duddon sonnets, and of the majestic description of moonrise upon the mountains in the fourteenth book of the *Prelude*, or that of the green linnet perched among the hazel trees:

> Yet seeming still to hover
> There where the flutter of his wings
> Upon his back and body flings
> Shadows and sunny glimmerings
> That cover him all over.

Of a kind with this is the wonderful picture given in the *Excursion* [1] of those towering peaks, the Langdale Pikes, vocal with the music of the torrent and the thunder and with those rarer harmonies that are not for the ear:

> In genial mood,
> While at our pastoral banquet thus we sate,
> Fronting the window of that little cell,
> I could not, ever and anon, forbear
> To glance an upward look on two huge Peaks,
> That from some other vale peered into this.
> 'Those lusty twins', exclaimed our host, 'if here
> It were your lot to dwell, would soon become
> Your prized companions. Many are the notes
> Which, in his tuneful course, the wind draws forth
> From rocks, woods, caverns, heaths and dashing shores;
> And well those lofty brethren bear their part
> In the wild concert—chiefly when the storm

[1] ii. 688–725.

Rides high; then all the upper air they fill
With roaring sound, that ceases not to flow,
Like smoke, along the level of the blast,
In mighty current; theirs, too, is the song
Of stream and headlong flood that seldom fails;
And, in the grim and breathless hour of noon,
Methinks that I have heard them echo back
The thunder's greeting. Nor have nature's laws
Left them ungifted with a power to yield
Music of finer tone; a harmony,
So do I call it, though it be the hand
Of silence, though there be no voice; –the clouds,
The mist, the shadows, light of golden suns,
Motions of moonlight, all come thither—touch,
And have an answer—thither come, and shape
A language not unwelcome to sick hearts
And idle spirits:—there the sun himself,
At the calm close of summer's longest day,
Rests his substantial orb;—between those heights
And on the top of either pinnacle,
More keenly than elsewhere in night's blue vault,
Sparkle the stars, as of their station proud.
Thoughts are not busier in the mind of man
Than the mute agents stirring there:—alone
Here do I sit and watch.'

The peculiar beauty of these passages could never have
been achieved, as so much fine poetry has been
achieved, by one who relied on mere native imagination,
fortified by a few stray hints of Nature. They come,
and only could have come, from one who had wooed her
with passion stronger and purer than a lover's, had
dwelt on her loveliness till it became part of himself, and
had drawn his inspiration from her soul.

In point of sheer perfection few, perhaps, of
Wordsworth's poems will compare with the lines
in which he associates the beauty of Nature with
the beauty of the young girl he loved. These lead
naturally to what is probably Meredith's most exquisite

poem, and they illustrate a certain fundamental unity of delight and love and beautiful expression existing between the two poets, despite fundamental divergences:

> She shall be sportive as the fawn,
> That wild with glee across the lawn
>   Or up the mountain springs;
> And hers shall be the breathing balm,
> And hers the silence and the calm
>   Of mute insensate things.
>
> The floating clouds their state shall lend
> To her; for her the willow bend;
>   Nor shall she fail to see
> Even in the motions of the Storm
> Grace that shall mould the Maiden's form
>   By silent sympathy.
>
> The stars of midnight shall be dear
> To her; and she shall lean her ear
>   In many a secret place
> Where rivulets dance their wayward round,
> And beauty born of murmuring sound
>   Shall pass into her face.[1]

We pass naturally from this to *Love in the Valley*, surely the most wondrous calendar ever penned, in which the poet sees Earth suffused throughout the year's changing months and seasons with the beauty of his beloved, and the glamour she awakens in his heart:

> Lovely are the curves of the white owl sweeping
>   Wavy in the dusk lit by one large star.
> Lone on the fir-branch, his rattle-note unvaried,
>   Brooding o'er the gloom, spins the brown evejar.
> Darker grows the valley, more and more forgetting;
>   So were it with me, if forgetting could be willed.
> Tell the grassy hollow that holds the bubbling well-
>   spring,
>   Tell it to forget the source that keeps it filled.

----

[1] 'Three years she grew in sun and shower.'

Stepping down the hill with her fair companions,
  Arm in arm, all against the raying West,
Boldly she sings, to the merry tune she marches,
  Brave is her shape, and sweeter unpossessed,
Sweeter, for she is what my heart first awaking
  Whispered the world was; morning light is she.
Love that so desires would fain keep her changeless,
  Fain would fling the net, and fain have her free.

Happy, happy time, when the white star hovers
  Low over dim fields fresh with bloomy dew,
Near the face of dawn, that draws athwart the darkness,
  Threading it with colour, like yewberries the yew.
Thicker crowd the shades as the grave East deepens,
  Glowing, and with crimson a long cloud swells.
Maiden still the morn is; and strange she is, and secret;
  Strange her eyes; her cheeks are cold as cold sea-
    shells.

With these last two perfect lines may be compared these
other not less exquisite ones:

  Lo, where the eyelashes of night are raised
  Yet lowly over morning's pure grey eyes:[1]

The poet's vision of his beloved in the moods of Nature
has a dim foreshadowing in the lines of Donne:

  I will not look upon the quickening sun,
  But straight her beauty to my sense shall run:
  The air shall note her soft, the fire most pure,
  Waters suggest her clear, and the earth sure.

A further example of sheer natural beauty unweighted
by any message to mankind, yet passing deep into their
hearts, is to be found in this sonnet from *Modern Love*,
in which the estranged husband and wife are tempor-
arily reunited on an evening of great beauty and
splendour:

  [1] *The Sage Enamoured and the Honest Lady*, end.

We saw the swallows gathering in the sky,
And in the osier-isle we heard them noise.
We had not to look back on summer joys,
Or forward to a summer of bright dye:
But in the largeness of the evening earth
Our spirits grew as we went side by side.
The hour became her husband and my bride.
Love that had robbed us so, thus blessed our dearth!
The pilgrims of the year waxed very loud
In multitudinous chatterings, as the flood
Full brown came from the West, and like pale blood
Expanded to the upper crimson cloud.
Love, that had robbed us of immortal things,
This little moment mercifully gave,
Where I have seen across the twilight wave
The swan sail with her young beneath her wings.

The same profound joy in Nature appears again as
intensely, though perhaps in less lovely form, in the
stanzas which describe the good physician Melampus—
stanzas which it is difficult to read without thinking
of their author and of Wordsworth, those good physicians
of human-kind, wise in the science of wood and stream
and hill:

With love exceeding a simple love of the things
   That glide in grasses and rubble of woody wreck;
Or change their perch on a beat of quivering wings
   From branch to branch, only restful to pipe and peck;
Or, bristled, curl at a touch their snouts in a ball;
   Or cast their web between bramble and thorny hook;
The good physician Melampus, loving them all,
   Among them walked, as a scholar who reads a book.

For him the woods were a home, and gave him the
      key
   Of knowledge, thirst for their treasures in herbs
      and flowers.
The secrets held by the creatures nearer than we
   To earth he sought, and the link of their life with
      ours:

And where alike we are, unlike where, and the veined
  Division, veined parallel, of a blood that flows
In them, in us, from the source by man unattained
  Save marks he well what the mystical woods disclose.

These stanzas breathe the very soul of the woodland,
and accurately symbolize Meredith's conception of
Nature as the revealer of herself to the sage and
poet. They recall the great chapter in the *Ordeal of
Richard Feverel*, where Richard, walking in black
despair and shame through the German woodland
in a torrent of rain, is recalled to life and hope and the
keen sense of fatherhood by the licking tongue of
a leveret which he has rescued in the forest. Meredith's
typical hero is Gower Woodseer, the passionate
Nature-lover ; and in this matter of sheer delight
in Nature's beauty, Meredith certainly brings to her
a pagan fierceness of adoration of quite a different order
from the high ethereal love with which Wordsworth
regarded her.

Many would doubtless prefer to sojourn in this land
of sheer beauty, to stray in the sunny meadows through
which Duddon passes before he plunges into the waste,
to linger in the fairy outskirts of the Woods of Westermain. But neither poet will by any means allow us to
do this. To each, Nature has a deeper meaning, and is
no mere beautiful but soulless odalisque. Earth is
something more than 'a meadow carpet for the dancing
hours'. First let us look at Meredith's teaching on this
point.

Meredith's philosophy of nature, as far as it affects the
conduct of man, may be summed up in the command—
Accept and Serve. Earth is always with him the
symbol of Nature, and throughout his poetry he hammers

home the lesson that man can only realize and perform
his true function by making the secret of Earth his own,
and living according to her teaching.   In one sense the
poet of evolution, he is always reminding us that it
is from Earth that we are sprung, and that though
the Race is ever going on from strength to strength, and
from height to height, such progress can only be realized
by forwarding Nature, and never by thwarting her.
Man must indeed reject the more vile and bestial
elements which he sees in her—one cannot insist too
strongly upon this aspect of Meredith's teaching.   But
having done this, he must take over the best that
Nature can give, and proceed to build on this basis.
This, the starting-point of Meredith's philosophy, may
seem a commonplace in an age whose thought has
been almost unconsciously determined by the discoveries
of Darwin : but it is in opposition to all mediaeval, and
to some modern, religion, and to all those theories
of philosophy—to that, for instance, of Schopenhauer—
which teach that spiritual welfare is only attainable
through asceticism.   For asceticism, Meredith had
all the hatred of William Blake, and in one passage he
classes the 'pinched ascetic' with the 'red sensualist' as
one who has utterly failed to grasp Nature's true
message.   He by whom the spirit of Earth is

misprised,
Brainlessly unrecognized,

is certain to fall into the slough of sentimentalism from
which spring the foul weeds of cowardice and vain
imagining.   On the contrary, only he who looked full
in Nature's face, who accepted her in all her manifestations of beauty and strength and apparent cruelty, could
know her message and strive for its fulfilment.   And

this acceptance of her must be not pessimistic, nor even
patient, but joyous and exultant : for if a man once entered
the Woods of Westermain, and looked upon Nature
with the right eyes, self-pity would cease within him,
and all things appurtenant to revelation would be done
for him.   He would see her, indeed, still red in tooth
and claw : but cruel though she were to the individual,
she was ever kindly to the Race : and it was in the Race
that the individual must learn from her to live the truer
and the larger life.   Once this truth is seized, Nature's
cloak of harshness falls away from her, and you

> Read her as no cruel Sphinx
> In the Woods of Westermain.[1]

For as we are told in *The Thrush in February*,

> But read her thought to speed the race,
>   And stars rush forth of blackest night,
> You chill not at a cold embrace
>   To come, nor dread a dubious might.

The beholder, in truth, becomes with the poet one of
those

> Who feel the Coming young as aye
>   Thrice hopeful on the ground we plough ;
> Alive for life, awake to die ;
>   One voice to cheer the seedling Now.

And at the last we are told in the following superb
stanzas :

> For love we Earth, then serve we all ;
>   Her mystic secret then is ours ;
> We fall, or view our treasures fall,
>   Unclouded, as beholds her flowers

> Earth, from a night of frosty wreck,
>   Enrobed in morning's mounted fire,
> When lowly, with a broken neck,
>   The crocus lays her cheek to mire.[2]

---

[1] *Woods of Westermain.*   [2] *The Thrush in February.*

To Wordsworth Nature gave intimations of something
that transcended her and was not herself.   To Meredith
she bore no message but that written plain upon her
face for all to read.   Man had no right to weave into
her his own vain imaginings or unwarrantable yearnings.
She was perfect in herself, a bride whose only dower
was her all-sufficing beauty.   No promise of personal
immortality must be sought in her—none, indeed, but
the psychically self-seeking would endeavour to find
such a promise.   Those who looked for a personal life
beyond the grave were those who were incapable of
the supreme altruism of merging their own life in that
of the Race, and serving it, regardless of future reward :

> I caught,
> With Death in me shrinking from Death,
> As cold from cold, for a sign
> Of the life beyond ashes ; I cast,
> Believing the vision divine,
> Wings of that dream of my Youth
> To the spirit beloved : 'twas unglassed
> On her breast, in her depths austere ;
> A flash through the mist, mere breath,
> Breath on a buckler of steel.[1]

Life, then, gave to Meredith none of the intimations of
immortality which she had given to Wordsworth : the
yearning for these was mere 'breath on a buckler of
steel' :

> These are our sensual dreams ;
> Of the yearning to touch, to feel
> The dark Impalpable sure,
> And have the Unveiled appear.[1]

These dreams and this yearning find no sanction in
Nature, for Nature has no sympathy for those who are

[1] *A Faith on Trial.*

not content with her message and crave more than she can offer : hence the poet's condemnation of the Legends, in which word he comprised most of the religions ; and of the Questionings, the vain speculations of an abstract philosophy :

> Harsh wisdom gives Earth, no more ;
> In one the spur and the curb :
> An answer to thoughts or deeds ;
> To the Legends, an alien look ;
> To the Questions, a figure of clay.[1]

And, again, he says, speaking of Earth :

> If he aloft for aid
> Imploring storms, her essence is the spur.
> His cry to heaven is a cry to her
> He would evade.[2]

But when the Legends and the Questionings have been rejected, where, we ask ourselves, are we to seek the satisfaction of the desire which most people occasionally feel—the desire for the final explanation of life, for the ideal, for the absolute ? Are we to stifle this desire, or can Nature fulfil it for us ? If it be not fulfilled, it is certain that materialism, and materialism alone, however apparently noble a form this may take, must be the sequel : and are we to conceive Meredith as the preacher of the gospel of matter ? To this question his answer is, most emphatically, No ! Meredith, consciously at least, is no materialist. On the contrary, he seeks Spirit everywhere : but Spirit must be sought *in* Nature, not beyond it, *through* the Real, not in the teeth of the Real ; and if the Real be sought strenuously, the Spiritual will come unasked. Thus he sings of Nature :

> We have but to see and hear,
> Crave we her medical herb.

[1] *A Faith on Trial.*   [2] *Earth and Man.*

For the road to her soul is the Real,
The root of the growth of man:
And the senses must traverse it fresh
With a love that no scourge shall abate
To reach the lone heights where we scan
In the mind's rarer vision this flesh,
In the charge of the Mother our fate;
Her law as the one common weal.[1]

All things, both real and spiritual, are contained in Earth, and beyond Earth we cannot go:

He who the reckoning sums
Finds nought in his hand save Earth.
Of Earth are we stripped or crowned.[1]

And it is Earth, and Earth alone, which leads to Spirit. Earth is

Spirit in her clods,
Footway to the God of Gods.[2]

(Earth, it must be again remarked, is throughout Meredith's poetry the symbol of Nature.)

And if we look Earth and Nature full in the face, and try to see in them the Real, we have in that very act made ourselves one with Reason—Reason, man's germinant fruit, the eternal foe of self, the prompter to service and self-sacrifice.   If man is one with Reason, the desire for supine comfort, for mere happiness, will cease within him, and he will know that

Wisdom is won of its fight,
The combat incessant.[1]

Nature's chosen were, to Meredith, her strong men—I had almost said her supermen—disciplined by her ruthless schooling into iron self-reliance. Thus, he says, speaking of a day of fierce wind:

[1] *A Faith on Trial.*   [2] *The Woods of Westermain.*

Look in the face of men who fare
Lock-mouthed, a match in lungs and thews
For this fierce angel of the air,
To twist with him and take his bruise.
That is the face beloved of old
Of Earth, young mother of her brood:
Nor broken for us shows the mould
When muscle is in mind renewed:
Though farther from her nature rude,
Yet nearer to her spirit's hold.[1]

Their fight must be waged to the death against all
that would thwart man's progress along Nature's path :—
against his own pessimism and sentimentalism, as against
any reversion to the more bestial elements of Nature,
which Meredith symbolized as 'the print of our fore-
father hoof'. The fighters must shun Precedents ;
Nature prompts them to Change

> as to promise of sun
> Till brain-rule splendidly towers,[2]

and her cry to them is ever:

> Keep the young generations in hail,
> And bequeath them no tumbled house![2]

'Live in thy offspring as I live in mine,'[3] she calls to
him ; and this he can only do by following ever 'the
lesson of the flesh',

> The lesson writ in red since first Time ran,
> A hunter hunting down the beast in man:
> That till the chasing out of its last vice,
> The flesh was fashioned but for sacrifice.[4]

He who has Reason will thus have transcended the

---

[1] *Hard Weather;* cf. *Foresight and Patience*—'Liker the clod
flaked by the driving plough', &c.
[2] *The Empty Purse.*   [3] *Earth and Man.*
[4] *France, December, 1870.*

senses and made himself their master: but he will not on this account have transcended Nature, nor will he dream of progress except along her path. But if he advance with Reason along that path, his progress will be steady and spiritual, undisturbed by vain cravings either for happiness or for the false ideal of a straying imagination:

> Flesh unto spirit must grow,
> Spirit raves not for a goal.
> Shapes in man's likeness hewn,
> Desires not; neither desires
> The Sleep or the Glory; it trusts;
> Uses my gifts, yet aspires;
> Dreams of a higher than it.[1]

And ever ready in Reason's Service was Laughter, the symbol of the Comic Spirit, which spoke with Nature's very voice, and was the great purifying spirit of the universe. 'A tear', said Blake, 'is an intellectual thing.' Meredith might have said the same of a laugh: for it was Laughter, based on a true knowledge of Nature's message, that must be used for the discomfiture of those who enter the Woods of Westermain with eyes shut to her beneficent purpose, interpreting all her processes in the light of their own sentimentalism and of the selfish personal sorrow which they have never learnt to lose in the joyous life of the Race; of these Meredith says:

> This Earth of the beautiful breasts,
> Shining up in all colours aflame,
> To them had visage of hags:
> A Mother of aches and jests;
> Soulless, heading a hunt
> Aimless except for the meal.[1]

[1] *A Faith on Trial.*

There would seem to be grave difficulties involved in
Meredith's philosophy.   One of its chief weaknesses is
surely his attempt to laugh out of court those who see
fundamental evil in Nature, instead of fundamental good.
Their case is far too strong for this to be done success-
fully; they speak with many voices, and are by no
means necessarily pessimistic in their general outlook.
One of them, Alfred de Vigny, contrasts the majesty
shown by man in his weakness and suffering with the
utter cruelty and insensibility which, as he believes,
underlie all Nature's beauty.   In the following passage
Nature boasts to Man of her ruthlessness:

> She saith, 'I am the vast impassive stage
>   That hath no thrill beneath its actors' tread;
> For all my emerald floors, my heritage
>   Of gold, my radiant statues' goodlihead,
>   Nor love is mine, nor mercy; o'er my head
> The ceaseless pageantry of life goes by,
> But I am deaf as are my heavens on high.

> 'I neither hear nor feel; in ruthless might
>   I mingle ant and man in common doom;
> Palace and grave are one before my sight,
>   From those I bear my face is wrapped in gloom:
>   Men call me Mother: but I am their tomb.
> My spring is deaf to man's adoring cries:
> My winter comes: his dearest droops and dies.

> 'Before thou wast, my face was fair and gay,
>   I sang my carol to the stars my peers,
> I held in heaven my immemorial way,
>   Stayed on the even axis of the spheres:
>   When thou art gone, throughout the eternal years
> I still shall hold my path with shining face
> Through the illimitable gulf of silent space.' [1]

[1] *La Maison du Berger.*

Then the poet addresses Nature:

Thus speaks to me her voice of gloom and dread,
    And in my heart I hate her then, and see
Our blood in all her waves, and all our dead
    Beneath her grass, feeding her every tree;
    And tell mine eyes that owned her witchery,
'Give not to her thy love, thy tears of pain,
Love what thou seest once, and ne'er again'.

Live, then, cold Nature; ay, live evermore:
    Live in our limbs and brows, if 'tis thy fate:
Live, goddess, in thy glory, and ignore
    Man's fleeting soul, whereon thy will should wait:
    More than thy reign and all its splendid state
The majesty of human grief can move
This heart of mine, that ne'er hath known thy love.

Vigny, of course, speaks with the voice of intense pessimism; and scarcely less fervid is the utterance of Matthew Arnold, in his sonnet entitled *In Harmony with Nature*: *To a Preacher*.

'In harmony with Nature?' Restless fool,
Who with such heat dost preach what were to thee,
When true, the last impossibility—
To be like Nature strong, like Nature cool!
Know, man hath all which Nature hath, but more,
And in that *more* lie all his hopes of good.
Nature is cruel, man is sick of blood;
Nature is stubborn, man would fain adore;
Nature is fickle, man hath need of rest;
Nature forgives no debt, and fears no grave;
Man would be mild, and with safe conscience blest.
Man must begin, know this, where Nature ends;
Nature and man can never be fast friends.
Fool, if thou canst not pass her, rest her slave!

It is an interesting comment upon Meredith's teaching, that the sentimentalist who is by him pilloried as Nature's chief foe appears in this sonnet of Arnold's as her undiscriminating adorer. Let us now listen to the outcry

against Nature of one who sought his ultimate consola-
tion in religion—Francis Thompson :

> Nature, poor stepdame, cannot slake my drouth;
> Let her, if she would owe me,
> Drop yon blue bosom-veil of sky, and show me
> The breasts o' her tenderness :
> Never did any milk of hers once bless
> My thirsting mouth.[1]

Science, too, has her word to say on the matter through
the mouth of Thomas Huxley, who, in his Romanes
Lecture on ' Evolution and Ethics ' remarks : ' As I have
already urged, the practice of that which is ethically best—
what we call goodness or virtue—involves a course of
conduct which in all respects is opposed to that which
leads to success in the cosmic struggle for existence.'
' Goodness ', says the Professor, ' repudiates the gladi-
atorial theory of the struggle for existence,' and after
noticing again the theory ' that the struggle for existence,
which has done such admirable work in cosmic nature,
must be equally beneficent in the ethical sphere ', he continues : ' Yet if what I have insisted on is true, if the
cosmic process has no sort of relation to moral ends, if
the imitation of it by man is inconsistent with the first
principles of ethics, what becomes of this surprising
theory ?
' Let us understand, once for all, that the ethical
progress of Society depends, not on imitating the cosmic
process, still less on running away from it, but on combating it.   It may seem an audacious proposal thus to pit the
microcosm against the macrocosm, and to set man to
subdue Nature to his higher ends ; but I venture to
think that the great intellectual difference between the

[1] *The Hound of Heaven.*

ancient times with which we have been occupied and
our day lies in the solid foundation we have acquired for
the hope that such an enterprise may meet with a certain
measure of success.'

So far Science : for Philosophy's indictment of
Nature we may turn to certain chapters of Schopenhauer's
World as Will and Idea, and Eduard von Hartmann's
Philosophy of the Unconscious.

These counts form a strong indictment, and must be
met seriously : they cannot be brushed scornfully aside,
as Meredith endeavours to brush them in his poem,
The Whimper of Sympathy, and in his second sonnet on
Shakespeare.   If evil is not the positive pole of existence,
as some have contended, there is still profound meaning
in Wordsworth's lines :

> Suffering is permanent, obscure and dark,
> And shares the nature of infinity.[1]

Nor can one completely dispose of the problem by
ordering the individual to lose himself utterly in the life
of the Race.   The duty of service and self-sacrifice in
the interest of one's kind is indeed the first principle
of practical conduct, and one that is inculcated by all
religion, as by all philosophy, worthy the name : and
the new and strenuous determination which Meredith
has given to this immemorial precept by attaching it to
the theory of Evolution is the inspiring force of his
philosophy and of some of his most powerful poetry.
But is such a noble ethical conception sufficient to explain
either certain processes of Nature or certain convictions
of the human consciousness ?   Furthermore, is the distinction a real one which Meredith draws in such poems

[1] *The Borderers*, Act III, ll. 409-10.

as *The Thrush in February* between the welfare of the individual and the welfare of his kind? Is that *Spirit* to which he so constantly appeals—the spirit, that is to say, of the Race—true spirit at all apart from the individual souls which compose the Race? The conception of such a spirit, one and permanent, seems necessarily to imply the idea of what is known as 'Race-Immortality': but is such Race-Immortality, implying as it does a persistence of the Race built up on the annihilation of the men and women who *are* the Race—immortality in anything but name? Can such a word be applied to a mere continuity or succession of separate and transitory personalities? Meredith says:

> Look with spirit past the sense,
> Spirit shines in permanence.[1]

But if there is no kind of future life for the individual, surely there is no such thing as Spirit, permanent and one, or Race-Immortality, and we are thrown back on the strong common sense of Huxley, who, after dealing with personal immortality, adds: 'I object still more to affirm that I look to a future life, when all that I mean is, that the influence of my sayings and doings will be more or less felt by a number of people after the physical components of that organism are scattered to the four winds. Throw a stone into the sea, and there is a sense in which it is true that the wavelets that spread around it have an effect through all space and time. Shall we say that the stone has a future life?'

Meredith constantly appeals to Spirit as the antithesis of Sense, and as the goal of human effort, yet he proceeds to declare his belief that the spirit of each human

[1] *The Woods of Westermain.*

being is inexorably doomed to annihilation, and is, therefore, entirely dependent on the material conditions of his body. This at the outset is surely an unwarrantable assumption, for no physical investigation has yet explained away Spirit, or proved it to be a mere appanage of Matter. And it is an assumption which does not satisfy Meredith himself. With the natural hatred of a great imaginative genius for the crudely materialistic explanation of the universe to which his original hypothesis would bring him, he appeals to a *permanent* Spirit belonging to a Race composed entirely of *mortal* and *transitory* men and women, a Spirit which belongs to all men, without properly belonging to any one of them. Surely such a hypothesis as this will not satisfy the consciousness or imagination of ordinary men and women. If men and women cease utterly to exist at death, we may still attribute to them so-called spirits which perish with them: but what we have surely no right to do is to assume the existence of an abstract Spirit, one and everlasting, which belongs to all of them, without properly belonging to any one of them. If, starting from the hypothesis that death is in all probability the end of all things, we then drag in Spirit to satisfy our instincts and explain the universe, we lay ourselves open to the admonition made by Valentine to Gretchen, 'Lass unsern Herrgott aus dem Spass'. It is surely impossible to conceive of permanent Spirit divorced from permanent personality. Either there is no immortality, or universal, single, and permanent Spirit, or there is some kind of immortality in which the individual has actual part.

We may look at the matter in another way. The individual may be prepared to sacrifice himself for the

Race with an unselfishness utterly regardless of the persistence of his own personality.   Often this self-sacrifice will take the form of death.   If death means absolute annihilation of the individual, it might well be claimed that the ethical value of the sacrifice is all the greater: but such a claim cannot fairly be used for the exaltation of Nature, who exacts the sacrifice.   It is the same with those who make no voluntary sacrifice, but merely surrender to Nature's claims.   If the individual survive death, even as a portion only of a universal Spirit in which she too has part, her beneficence could still be established, in spite of the ruthlessness with which she had swept him from life.   But it surely cannot be established on the basis of that utter annihilation of personality which Meredith supposes.   The difficulty is not met by saying that the supreme good of those who *are* can only be attained in the existence of those who *are to be*; for this is to seek the individual's highest being in the mirage of an ever-receding futurity in which no individual can ever have part.   The very possibility of the individual's finding a positive supreme good in the existence of his successors implies a continuation of consciousness, whether personal or universal, and hence a continuation of existence.   No race composed solely of individuals can realize the postulated good by the waste or suffering or destruction of its component parts, unless this waste, destruction, and suffering be given deeper meaning for the individual.   The great difficulty—and it seems to me the great weakness—of Meredith's ethical conception is that under it the individual becomes a mere means, instead of being, as in the Kantian ethic, an end in himself; it is true that the end to which he is made a means is with Meredith

a noble one; but this is not enough; for, in the words
of Wordsworth,

> Our life is turned
> Out of her course, wherever man is made
> An offering or a sacrifice, a tool
> Or implement, a passive thing employed
> As a brute mean, without acknowledgement
> Of common right or interest in the end.[1]

The objection cannot be disposed of by such a superb
piece of special pleading as that made by Mr. G. M.
Trevelyan in his book on *Meredith's Poetry and
Philosophy*. The matter is not merely one of individual
happiness, for the highest form of self-expression
is often reached by the negation of this: the question
is rather whether the service and self-sacrifice of the
individual have essential and permanent *meaning* for
him. Are they, in fact, the only means by which he
attains true personality at all, or do they merely
culminate, as Meredith would have us believe, in
a sublime form of self-annihilation? That they do not
culminate in this has been the contention of many
of the world's greatest speculative thinkers, many of
whom have held the extinction of the individual to imply
absorption in a higher unity or totality. It is not our
present purpose to consider whether such a unity,
implicit in Nature, and at once transcending and
explaining her, is one which commends itself to the
consciousness of men, as Wordsworth certainly thought
it did. It is open to any one to deny the existence of
such a conception; but those who do deny it must not
shirk the consequences; unless such a unity can be
found as will give a deeper meaning to evil and waste

[1] *Excursion*, ix. 113-18.

and suffering—such a meaning, for instance, as that
attached to them by Hegel—there is no valid answer
to the indictment of Huxley and Arnold, at least as
regards that Nature whose symbol is the Woods of
Westermain ; and there is probably none as regards
that wider Nature which includes the whole universe
and man. There is sublime beauty in the cry of
Meredith :

> Into the breast that gives the rose
> Shall I with shuddering fall?[1]

But there is still greater sublimity, due just to the
consciousness of this transcendental unity, in the answer
of Faust, just before his descent to the lower world, to
the cynical promptings of Mephistopheles :

In deinem ' Nichts ' hoff' ich das All zu finden.

The bearing of all this on Nature is best expressed
in the words of Hegel: 'There is no prospect of
returning from the uncultured earnestness and troubled
sensibility of the modern views of Nature to the
joyousness and purity of the Greek modes of regarding it, except in one way, and that is by restoring the
lost identity through speculation, and once more
merging the division in a higher potency.'   Let us see
if we can find this potency in Wordsworth.

When we consider Wordsworth's poetry in this
aspect, the divergence between it and Meredith's
becomes at once clear and fundamental.   If Meredith
may be called in some sense the poet of Evolution,
Wordsworth may be called, with similar restrictions,
the poet of Philosophy.   His spiritual kinship with the
great German metaphysical thinkers of his age has

---

[1] *Ode to the Spirit of Earth in Autumn.*

been brought out in a recently-published lecture by
Dr. A. C. Bradley, which, read in connexion with
two of his Oxford lectures, represents the most
profound and luminous study of Wordsworth with
which I am acquainted. 'All Romanticism', says
Lanson, 'is penetrated with metaphysical quiverings,
and this is its main glory.' Wordsworth, the most
deeply romantic of all poets, is no philosopher only
because he is more than a philosopher. Although
there is ordered thought throughout his writings, his
highest poetry arrives at conclusions akin to those of
Kant and Hegel by the short cut of inspiration, instead of
using the hard and long road of rigorous logical reasoning. For light upon this inspiration we must go back
again to his own utterances.

There had been a time in his life, he tells us, when
he had looked upon Nature with the presumptuous
eye of mere artistic dilettantism: he had savoured
fastidiously

> The winds,
> And roaring waters and the lights and shades
> That marched and countermarched about the hills
> In glorious apparition.[1]

He had been

> even in pleasure pleased
> Unworthily, disliking here, and there
> Liking, by rules of mimic art transferred
> To things above all art.[2]

Even when he had avoided this dilettantism, he had
still often regarded Nature merely with the physical
eye which takes in the outer show of things, and is
blind to

> The affections and the spirit of the place.[3]

---

[1] *Prelude*, xii. 96-8.   [2] *Ibid.*, xii. 109-12.   [3] *Ibid.*, xii. 120.

At this period he would have been moved[1] to draw
Peele Castle but with the artist's hand,

> And add the gleam,
> The light that never was on sea or land,
> The consecration, and the poet's dream.

It was of this season, too, that he could say:

> The sounding cataract
> Haunted me like a passion: the tall rock,
> The mountain, and the deep and gloomy wood,
> Their colours and their forms, were then to me
> An appetite; a feeling and a love,
> That had no need of a remoter charm,
> By thought supplied, nor any interest
> Unborrowed from the eye.[2]

But he was not long to remain thus. During his
early manhood he had undergone a profound spiritual
crisis, the result in great measure of his disillusionment
with the French Revolution, and with the sterile
philosophy of William Godwin. From the gloomy
despondency of this period he was rescued by the
guidance of his sister Dorothy, the companionship
of Coleridge, and the deeper understanding of Nature
to which he was brought by their influence. As he
grew in years and came to scan Nature more piercingly,
as, after his brother John's death, he came to read the
book of life with the gloss of suffering, then

> The intellectual power through words and things
> Went sounding on, a dim and perilous way,

and brought him into depths where he had never yet
moved. The cataract became more to him than a
passion; it became a Vision Beautiful, a symbol of

---

[1] Cf. Sir Walter Raleigh, *Wordsworth*, p. 108.
[2] *Lines Composed above Tintern Abbey*, 76–82.

scarce utterable things. His vision, like that of Blake, was henceforth, as it had been in the beginning, ' twofold always ', and he looked with contempt on ' the blind, mechanical talent, that walks while the soul sleeps, with the mere activity of a blind somnambulism '. He regained once more the mood of his youth—the mood in which Jacob Böhme gazed on a green field before Görlitz till he saw the essences, use and properties of the herbs and grasses, and, through them, the mysteries of creation—the mood in which, as Wordsworth tells us :

> with an eye made quiet by the power
> Of harmony and the deep power of joy,
> We see into the life of things.[1]

It is thus that he can say in words which are the final expression of his thought and poetry :

> I have felt
> A presence that disturbs me with the joy
> Of elevated thoughts ; a sense sublime
> Of something far more deeply interfused,
> Whose dwelling is the light of setting suns,
> And the round ocean and the living air,
> And the blue sky, and in the mind of man :
> A motion and a spirit, that impels
> All thinking things, all objects of all thought,
> And rolls through all things.[2]

The same thought is expressed in the *Address to Kilchurn Castle* :

> Oh ! there is life that breathes not ; Powers there are
> That touch each other to the quick in modes
> Which the gross world no strength hath to perceive,
> No soul to dream of.

This sense of a great unity which comprised both Nature and himself, explained both her and him, and

---

[1] *Lines Composed above Tintern Abbey*, 46-8. [2] *Ibid.*, 92-101.

it also explained the profound feeling—some say of
infinity—which all who have sought and loved Nature
have sometimes felt in her presence. The power, says
Wordsworth,

> which Nature thus
> To bodily sense exhibits, is the express
> Resemblance of that glorious faculty
> That higher minds bear with them as their own.[1]

It was only the man who had thus heard the mighty
stream of tendency, and looked with the eyes of the
Spirit into Nature's soul, who could hope to recapture
something of the glory which, as we are told in the
Ode on some Intimations of Immortality, the new-born
child brings with him from the unknown world, and
which, in most men, shimmers gradually into nothingness under the beat of the world's garish light.

It is thus that he treats of Nature the Revealer.
Of Nature the Healer, he tells us :

> Therefore let the moon
> Shine on thee in thy solitary walk ;
> And let the misty mountain-winds be free
> To blow against thee ; and in after years,
> When these wild ecstasies shall be matured
> Into a sober pleasure ; when thy mind
> Shall be a mansion for all lovely forms,
> Thy memory be as a dwelling place
> For all sweet sounds and harmonies ; oh ! then,
> If solitude, or fear, or pain, or grief
> Should be thy portion, with what healing thoughts
> Of tender joy wilt thou remember me
> And these my exhortations ![2]

As both Nature and man are informed by the same
great Spirit, it is Wordsworth's constant teaching that
man, when he beholds her, is not less creative of her

[1] *Prelude* xiv. 85-90.
[2] *Lines Composed above Tintern Abbey*, 134-46.

than she has been of him. The mind to him was no
mere 'pensioner on outward forms', for he tells us—

> Finally, whate'er
> I saw or heard or felt was but a stream
> That flowed into a kindred stream: a gale
> Confederate with the current of the soul,
> To speed my voyage.[1]

(In the subjective idealism of some of his utterances on
this point Wordsworth seems almost to speak with the
voice of Fichte, even as he speaks with the very voice
of Immanuel Kant—whom we know he had read
closely—in the great passage on Duty in the Fourth
Book of the *Excursion*.[2])

Of this creative power he says:

> An auxiliar light
> Came from my mind which on the setting sun
> Bestowed new splendour: the melodious birds,
> The fluttering breezes, fountains that run on,
> Murmuring so sweetly in themselves, obeyed
> A like dominion, and the midnight storm
> Grew darker-in the presence of my eye.[3]

It is impossible here to go into the metaphysical
aspect of this creative faculty of man, this unity of
the perceiver with the perceived, the belief in which
is, in one form or another, an integral part of all
idealistic philosophy. It has been emphasized here
because it lies at the heart of Wordsworth's conception
of the relation between man and Nature, and of his
belief that the deep response which each made to the

---

[1] *Prelude*, vi. 743-6.

[2] *Excursion*, iv. 70-122; cf. *Prelude* x. 182-90; and *The Ode to Duty*.

[3] *Prelude*, ii. 368-74; cf. *Prelude*, i. 33-5; ii. 255-60; iii. 133-5; xiv. 94-5.

other is a sign that the two are ultimately one expression of a supreme principle.

In the light of these considerations, it is not
wonderful that in his essential interpretation of Nature
Wordsworth must differ utterly from Meredith.   To
the latter, as to Peter Bell, a primrose by the river's
brim was still a yellow primrose—the loveliest nursling,
doubtless, of the Valley Beautiful or the Woods of
Westermain ; a flower instinct with Nature's message,
and radiant with her glory, yet having no part in
anything which rose above her or informed her with
infinity; an emblem, not a symbol; a thing still physical, supplying to man rather a sublime text than
a transcendent revelation.   To Wordsworth, such a
flower had part in something far more deeply interfused :
it was one with what Plato called the Soul of the
World, and with something higher than that Soul :
it was one with the soul of man : nay, it was Soul itself,
and took delight in its existence.   ' It is my faith ', says
Wordsworth, 'that every flower enjoys the air it
breathes.'   This conception may be attacked by those
who would 'peep and botanize upon their mother's
grave', as by less ruthless investigators ; but what
these writers must not do, as Professor Raleigh has
warned them, is deny that Wordsworth believed what
he said, or attribute to his pleasant fancy what he has
told us is his faith.

A glance at those whom Meredith and Wordsworth,
respectively, consider Nature's chosen children will
throw further light on their different interpretations
of her.   To Meredith, as we have seen, these chosen
ones had been the strong men battling, lock-mouthed,
with the buffetings of the gale, and schooled into iron

self-reliance by Nature's stern discipline. Wordsworth
in a passage of the *Excursion* gives full value to such
discipline, and again, in the *Prelude*, after dismissing
the worldlings, he praises those who

> are their own upholders, to themselves
> Encouragement and energy and will.[1]

And in another passage he says:

> Stern was the face of Nature: we rejoiced
> In that stern countenance: for our souls thence drew
> A feeling of their strength.[2]

He thus knew Nature in this aspect through and
through; but here again he must needs go deeper, and,
to his mind, Nature's highest were not her strivers, but
her simple and silent seers, those who, by much musing
on her processes, saw deep into her heart.   These he
contrasts with the eloquent worldlings :—

> Others too
> There are among the walks of homely life
> Still higher, men for contemplation framed,
> Shy and unpractised in the strife of phrase;
> Meek men, whose very souls perhaps would sink
> Beneath them, summoned to such intercourse :
> Theirs is the language of the heavens, the power,
> The thought, the image, and the silent joy:
> Words are but under-agents in their souls;
> When they are grasping with their greatest strength
> They do not breathe among them.[3]

And how does Wordsworth deal with the problem of
evil in Nature?   He does not, as a matter of fact, deal
with this aspect of her expressly at all, and even, as

---

[1] *Prelude*, xiii. 262-3.

[2] '*Bleak season was it, turbulent and wild*'—Knight's Edition
(Macmillan), vol. ii, p. 121.

[3] *Prelude*, xiii. 269-75; cf. *Excursion*, vi. 179 seq.

many of his critics have noticed, shows a tendency to shrink from discussing it. In his age the theory of the struggle for survival had not made its way insensibly into the minds of men as it has among ourselves since the day of Darwin. This, however, is hardly a sufficient explanation of his attitude, for it would apply also to Vigny, whose terrible indictment of Nature has been already quoted. Whatever be the explanation, it is surely true that, in the words of Professor Bradley, ' Wordsworth yields here and there too much to a tendency to contrast the happiness, innocence, and harmony of Nature with the unrest, misery, and sin of man '.

Yet when he came to the world of men and women, Wordsworth was in no sense blind to evil and suffering, and if it be true that he did 'avert his ken from half of human fate', that half was certainly not the one which comprised the miserable and the outcast. In such poems as *Ruth, Michael, The Vision of Margaret, Simon Lee,* and innumerable others, as well as throughout the first and intermediate books of the *Excursion,* he shows that he has gone into the depth of things, has read the innermost meaning of human sorrow, and has felt in himself and others the meaning of his own tremendous lines :

> Suffering is permanent, obscure and dark,
> And shares the nature of infinity.

It is clear that the man who could write and feel this couplet had nothing in him of the morbid optimism, the moral photophobia, which smarts and shrinks and turns away when the fierce light of truth is flashed into his soul and into the forlorn and terrible places of the world. No detailed account can here be given of Wordsworth's conception of sorrow and its meaning. As Professor Bradley has shown, it seems akin to that of Hegel, and realizes, at least implicitly, that evil is the necessary correlative of good, and that alone through evil, the negation, can good, the actuality, have positive being. It is Wordsworth's constant teaching that the soul, by her own effort, can wring good out of evil :

> Within the soul a faculty abides
> That with interpositions, which would hide
> And darken, so can deal that they become
> Contingencies of pomp; and serve to exalt
> Her native brightness. As the ample moon,
> In the deep stillness of a summer even,
> Rising behind a thick and lofty grove,
> Burns, like an unconsuming fire of light,
> In the green trees; and, kindling on all sides
> Their leafy umbrage, turns the dusky veil
> Into a substance glorious as her own,
> Yea, with her own incorporated, by power
> Capacious and serene. Like power abides
> In man's celestial spirit; virtue thus
> Sets forth and magnifies herself; thus feeds
> A calm, a beautiful, and silent fire,
> From the encumbrances of mortal life,
> From error, disappointment—nay, from guilt;
> And sometimes, so relenting justice wills,
> From palpable oppressions of despair.[1]

And again he tells us—

> Nor all the misery forced upon my sight,
> Misery not lightly passed, but sometimes scanned
> Most feelingly, could overthrow my trust
> In what we *may* become.[2]

Most profound of all is the passage on the meaning of sorrow in the Fourth Book of the *Excursion*,[3] where the

---

[1] *Excursion*, iv. 1058-77 ; cf. *Prelude*, x. 465 seq.
[2] *Prelude*, viii. 647-50.　　[3] *Excursion*, iv. 140-96.

prostration of grief for what is lost is attributed, not to the mere 'weight of anguish unrelieved', but to the soul's inability to realize the transfigured vision that has once been granted it.

In the light of this it is, I think, a fair assumption that he who felt this deeper meaning in evil, waste, and suffering as seen in man, would, if the case against Nature had been put to him by her enemies, have answered it as he had answered the previous difficulty and have shown that it had a deeper meaning for the individual than one of mere utility to the Race.

In any case, it now becomes obvious that Wordsworth regarded Nature not merely as a being in some sense external to man—a being beneficent to her favourites, and ruthless to her weaklings—but as being in essence one with him, and part of the transcendent unity in which he was comprised. Hence, there could be no antithesis between the individual and the Race, for all individuals were comprised in a higher totality, which rendered any such antithesis meaningless. To Wordsworth, duty had a more deep-seated and positive sanction than she had to Meredith. He did not confine man's function to promoting the continuance of a succession of other finite personalities, with whom he was connected by no real or universal bond of Spirit, and in whose progress he could have no permanent part ; nor did he limit the essential value of existence, as did Meredith, to the strong ones of this earth ; but believing as firmly as ever did Meredith in that spirit of self-sacrifice to one's kind which he celebrates in the *Ode to Duty*, he gave to that spirit a profounder meaning, and attached the individual to the force through which the most ancient heavens are fresh and strong.

Hence, Spirit was not one thing in the transitory individual, and another in that persisting aggregate called the Race ; it was immanent in each man and woman, and was the bond which attached them to one another, as to the immortal personalities which had passed beyond time and space.   There is thus none of the conflict between the unity and permanence of Spirit on the one hand, and the transitoriness of the individual on the other, which is, as I have tried to show, one of the chief difficulties—it seems to me one of the chief weaknesses—of Meredith's philosophy.

Although Spirit, with Wordsworth, had part in eternity, it still spoke with sovereign authority to the humblest, for Duty, the supreme lesson of Nature, was not

> difficult, abstruse, and dark,
> Hard to be won, and only by a few.

On the contrary, its meaning was obvious to the lowliest, and written plain on Nature's face for all to read :

> The primal duties shine aloft like stars,
> The charities that soothe and heal and bless
> Are scattered at the feet of Man like flowers.[1]

Such would seem to be Wordsworth's intuition of Nature. His message will certainly not bear conviction to those who are not already prepared to receive it, for it is true of him, as of his own poet, that

> You must love him ere to you
> He will seem worthy of your love.

While his reading of Nature is akin to that of the deepest speculative philosophy, to many it will seem to supply a profound need of the human consciousness, and in this reason alone to find its fullest proof and

[1] *Excursion*, ix. 238-40.

sanction. There is profound truth here, as elsewhere, in the lines of Blake :—

> He who replies to words of doubt
> Doth put the light of knowledge out ;
> A riddle or the cricket's cry,
> Is to doubt a fit reply.

Although Wordsworth walks with Meredith along the high road of Reason, through the wondrous Woods of Westermain, as far as cautious Reason will take him, there comes a time when the two part company, and Wordsworth takes the high and difficult path that leads from the forest to the mountain peak.   Those who cannot breathe this air will fall back with relief on the sure and noble faith of Meredith, which in its practical bearing has, like his finest poetry, deep value for all men and for all time.   But there will be always many who will feel a deeper need ; and these will return again and again to Wordsworth, who embodies the highest tradition of the world's philosophic thought in a form far more human, simple, and exquisite than that used by any philosopher.   We have here two great poets ; let us give thanks for each after his kind.